The Disciple Maker's Handbook will show you the foundational principle in order to be unleashed as a disciple maker right where you are.

—**Kyle Idleman,** Author of *Not a Fan* and Teaching Pastor Southeast Christian Church, Louisville, KY

I love what Bobby and Josh have done. *The Disciple Maker's Handbook* will help any believer live out their God-given destiny and fulfill God's purposes on earth.

—**Doug Nuenke,** US President of the Navigators

Bobby and Josh take the principles from *DiscipleShift* and describe how everyday Christians can live them out. I recommend almost any book Bobby writes or helps write.

—**Jim Putman,** Pastor and coauthor of *DiscipleShift*
(with Bobby Harrington and Robert Coleman)

I really like this book. It is so easy to use, to get through, to find what you want. Bobby and Josh have done a great job of presenting a clear and compelling case for making disciples.

—**Bill Hull,** Leader and Cofounder of The Bonhoeffer Project,
author of *Conversion & Discipleship* and *The Christian Leader*

This book is a beautiful guide for making disciple makers. It is simple, practical, down-to-earth, and Christ-centered. I commend it to everyone.

—**Robert Coleman,** Author of *The Master Plan of Evangelism*, Distinguished Senior Professor of Discipleship and Evangelism, Gordon-Conwell Theological Seminary, and founding member of the Lausanne Committee on World Evangelization

You can't go wrong if you help people become more like Jesus. Here disciple makers Bobby Harrington and Josh Patrick help us find our way back to a more authentic following of our Lord.

—**Alan Hirsch,** Award-winning author on missional movements, leadership, and discipleship. www.alanhirsch.org

Bobby and Josh have provided a great tool in *The Disciple Maker's Handbook* that I believe will move us from merely studying and talking about discipleship to becoming disciple makers.

—**Jeff Vanderstelt,** Author of *Saturate* and *Gospel Fluency*; Visionary Leader of Saturate and the Soma Family of Churches; Lead Visionary Pastor of Doxa Church

The Disciple Maker's Handbook is an important tool for doing the church's most important work!

—**Dave Ferguson,** Lead Pastor of Community Christian Church, lead visionary of NewThing

The Disciple Maker's Handbook is a must read for all church planters and church multiplication leaders. This is not just another theoretical guide, but a vitally important practical framework for anyone seeking to be part of Jesus' Great Commission to make disciples!

—**Todd Wilson,** Founder and Director of the Exponential Church Planting Conference and Exponential Network

The process of discipleship involves the whole of our lives, not just our theology. In *The Disciple Maker's Handbook* Harrington and Patrick have provided the body of Christ with a holistic and practical tool for discipleship. It's my prayer that we use it for the glory of God as we make disciples from every ethnicity.

—**D. A. Horton,** Author and Pastor of Reach Fellowship in North Long Beach, CA, and Chief Evangelist for the Urban Youth Workers Institute

Bobby Harrington and Josh Patrick have taken the guesswork out of beginning a disciple-making movement. The book is extremely practical because it's birthed out of years of investing in others.

—**Robby Gallaty,** PhD, Senior Pastor of Long Hollow Baptist Church and author of *Growing Up, Rediscovering Discipleship,* and *The Forgotten Jesus*

The Disciple Maker's Handbook is a helpful and practical guide for those of us who want to actually leave behind a legacy of changed lives. I encourage you to read it carefully.

—**Larry Osborne,** Pastor and author, North Coast Church, Vista, CA

This is a practical and powerful resource for making students of Jesus.

—**Jonathan Storment,** Patheos blogger and Preaching Minister at Highland Church of Christ

In an age of religious boredom, church hopping, and spiritual consumerism. Bobby and Josh have written an outstanding resource for those who long for more. I can't recommend this book to you highly enough.

—**Scott Sauls,** Senior Pastor of Christ Presbyterian Church in Nashville, TN, and author of *Jesus Outside the Lines* and *Befriend*

If you are looking for a clear and compelling book on disciple making, then you have found it! I highly recommend this book!

—**Craig Etheredge,** Lead Pastor of First Colleyville Church, DiscipleFIRST ministries

Filled with clear transferable principles, biblical wisdom, keen insight, and practical tools . . . you will find this an easy and enjoyable read. I highly commend it to you.

—**Dr. Dann Spader,** Founder of Sonlife; President, Global Youth Initiative

The challenge we face in our church today is that everyone wants to be a disciple, but not make disciples! *The Disciple Maker's Handbook* helps every follower of Jesus see not only the why, but the how to making disciples.

—**Shelly Juskiewicz,** Pastor of Community Life & Leadership Development,
Mariners Church, CA

My friends, Bobby Harrington and Josh Patrick, have created a handy reference to equip pastors and their flocks to make disciple makers! *The Disciple Maker's Handbook* provides fresh insights and everyday applications.

—**Dave Buehring,** Lionshare Founder and President

Bobby and Josh have given us a helpful, inspiring framework for disciple making—so steal their hard work and jump-start your church's disciple-making system!

—**Alex Absalom,** Missional coach, author, and speaker—dandelionresourcing.com

As a denominational leader I am always looking for just the right tool to put in the hands of large numbers of pastors and leaders. This handbook is the perfect resource to equip them for their ministry's most important work—disciple making!

—**Larry Walkemeyer,** Lead Pastor of Light and Life Christian Fellowship,
Superintendent of FMCSC

This book is a tool that really helps Christ-followers understand how and why we make disciples. I hope it inspires you as much as Bobby's life has inspired me!

—**Dr. Kennon Vaughan,** Senior Pastor of Harvest Church,
President of Downline Ministries

This is truly a handbook for disciplers. If you have a heart for discipling others, this is your resource!

—**Shawn Lovejoy,** Founder and CEO of CourageToLead.com

This book is an amplifier for the very words of Jesus, to awaken God's church to its intended purpose.

—**Andy Savage,** @andysavage, Teaching Pastor at Highpoint Church, Memphis, TN

Bobby and Josh hit the nail with their heads in *The Disciple Maker's Handbook*. It is not a book you read just once, but one you keep on your shelf and read again and again.

—**Roy Moran,** Author of *Spent Matches: Igniting a Signal Fire for the Spiritually Dissatisfied*

This book is a must-read, not only for those interested in the discipline of making disciples, but for all Christians, since making disciples is a call to all.

—**Brandon Grant,** Lead Pastor of Rise City Church, San Diego, CA

This book is highly recommended. It's full of many inspiring and practical ideas based on experience, shared wisdom, and the Word of God. Buy the book!

—**Henry Kriete,** Lead Pastor, Discovery Church, Kelowna, Canada

The Disciple Maker's Handbook is an intentional, transparent, and empowering resource that offers hands-on ways to develop meaningful relationships to grow disciples in the Christian faith.

—**Amy Alexander,** Licensed Marriage and Family Therapist (LMFT) and Executive Director of The Refuge Center for Counseling

Bobby Harrington and Josh Patrick have written a compelling book on discipleship. I love their emphasis on relationships as the essential matrix of following Jesus and their willingness to challenge old paradigms while forging new ones. Most of all, Bobby and Josh are in the trenches of ministry trying to do this stuff. In this book you won't find any lofty ideas that haven't been implemented; only tried and true practices that will help shape the church to become the radical band of Christ-followers we are called to be.

—**Preston Sprinkle,** Speaker, teacher, and author of *Go: Returning Discipleship to the Front Lines of Faith*

Without a doubt, Bobby and Josh provided us with a valuable resource in *The Disciple Maker's Handbook*. They remind us that making and training disciples is not the latest fad, but rather a tried and true model that Jesus employed. If you desire to see people move from unbelief to belief and then to maturity, you have found the right resource. I wholeheartedly recommend this book to you.

—**Randy Pope,** Pastor of Perimeter Church, Johns Creek, GA

THE
DISCIPLE MAKER'S
HANDBOOK

7 ELEMENTS OF A DISCIPLESHIP LIFESTYLE

BOBBY HARRINGTON

JOSH PATRICK

A Discipleship.org Resource

ZONDERVAN®

For Chad and Rachel: God blessed us with a beloved son and a godly woman who is his wonderful wife.
—*Bobby*

For my wife, Joni: Apart from Jesus himself, you are the clearest demonstration of God's grace in my life; and my daughters, Lilly, Joy, and Sarah: You make my heart overflow with gratitude and joy! —*Josh*

ZONDERVAN

The Disciple Maker's Handbook
Copyright © 2017 by Bobby Harrington and Josh Patrick

This title is also available as a Zondervan ebook.

Requests for information should be addressed to:
Zondervan, *3900 Sparks Drive SE, Grand Rapids, Michigan 49546*

Library of Congress Cataloging-in-Publication Data

Names: Harrington, Bobby, 1958- author. | Patrick, Josh, 1979- author.
Title: The disciple maker's handbook : seven elements of a discipleship lifestyle / Bobby Harrington,
     Josh Patrick.
Description: Grand Rapids, Michigan : Zondervan, [2016]
Identifiers: LCCN 2016038229 | ISBN 9780310525271 (softcover)
Subjects: LCSH: Discipling (Christianity) | Evangelistic work.
Classification: LCC BV4520 .H3737 2016 | DDC 253--dc23 LC record available at https://lccn.loc
     .gov/2016038229

The Bible versions quoted in this book are listed on page 8, which therefore becomes a part of this copyright page.

Any Internet addresses (websites, blogs, etc.) and telephone numbers in this book are offered as a resource. They are not intended in any way to be or imply an endorsement by Zondervan, nor does Zondervan vouch for the content of these sites and numbers for the life of this book.

Published in association with the literary agency of Mark Sweeney & Associates, Bonita Springs, Florida 34135.

Cover design: Tim Green / FaceOut Studio
Interior background imagery: (c) Sociologas/Shutterstock
Interior design: Kait Lamphere

Printed in the United States of America

17 18 19 20 21 22 23 24 25 26 27 /DHV/ 20 19 18 17 16 15 14 13 12 11 10 9 8 7 6 5 4 3 2

CONTENTS

BIBLE VERSIONS

All Scripture quotations, unless otherwise indicated, are taken from The Holy Bible, New International Version®, NIV®. Copyright © 1973, 1978, 1984, 2011 by Biblica, Inc.® Used by permission of Zondervan. All rights reserved worldwide. www.Zondervan.com. The "NIV" and "New International Version" are trademarks registered in the United States Patent and Trademark Office by Biblica, Inc.®

Scripture quotations marked ESV are taken from the ESV® Bible (The Holy Bible, English Standard Version). Copyright © 2001 by Crossway, a publishing ministry of Good News Publishers. Used by permission. All rights reserved.

Scripture quotations marked NLT are taken from the Holy Bible, New Living Translation. Copyright © 1996, 2004, 2007, 2013 by Tyndale House Foundation. Used by permission of Tyndale House Publishers, Inc., Carol Stream, Illinois 60188. All rights reserved.

Scripture quotations marked MSG are taken from *The Message*. Copyright © by Eugene H. Peterson 1993, 1994, 1995, 1996, 2000, 2001, 2002. Used by permission of NavPress. All rights reserved. Represented by Tyndale House Publishers Inc.

ACKNOWLEDGMENTS

We want to start by acknowledging and saying that Ryan Pazdur of Zondervan has been incredibly good to work with on this project. We may not have written or completed it without him. We highly value our relationship with him in this project and other discipleship.org projects, past and future. Mark Sweeney also deserves our warm thank you.

A very special thanks to our wonderful elders at Harpeth Christian Church who believe in and support disciple making in our church and globally through discipleship.org—David Sanders, Mike Shake, Tony Dupree, and Ed Kaeser—and also to a couple of great women on our staff team who reviewed this book several times: Michelle Eagle and Kathy Cawley.

We wrote this book with a team of national discipleship leaders giving us regular input. First, Todd Wilson, Robert Coleman, Bill Hull, Josh Shank, Leon Drenan, Alan Hirsch, and Jim Putman helped Bobby identify and clarify the seven elements from Jesus's ministry. Then we continued to work through and clarify the principles and their application, including in a national discipleship forum on six of them in the fall of 2014, where discipleship.org and Exponential featured Francis Chan, Jeff Vanderstelt, and K.P. Yohannan, with Bill Hull, Jim Putman, and Robert Coleman discussing them. Then folks like Robby Gallaty, Alex Absalom, Kennon Vaughn, Pat Morley, Dann Spader, Luke Yetter, and Randy Pope and others also spoke into this frame work and our definitions.

We now hope and trust that we now have

a framework for a broad disciple making movement in North America and beyond.

■ ■ ■

I (Bobby) cannot express warmly enough my love and affection for my wife, Cindy. She especially supported me through the many extra days and nights of writing that the special last-minute circumstances of the situations with this book required. She is one special godly lady.

■ ■ ■

I (Josh) am incredibly grateful for my youth minister, Lonnie Jones, who always seemed to show up at just the right time. His investment of time and energy forever altered the direction of my life. After I walked away from law school and decided to go to seminary, I had the privilege of being discipled by two of the best and most brilliant men I've ever known. They are Harold Shank and Chris Altrock. I'll never stop praising God for the four years we spent together. They continually pointed me to Jesus and called out the good in me. When I grow up, I aspire to be like them.

■ ■ ■

Bobby and Josh also wish to acknowledge Everett Huffard and Rick Oster as two men who loved and discipled us at Harding Graduate school (in different decades), and we wish time, distance, and other things would have allowed us to have been closer to them in these most recent years.

INTRODUCTION

Do you want your life to count? Do you want to look back and say that you made the biggest difference possible?

Most Christians want to devote their lives to something significant. Deep inside they want to make some kind of difference in the world, to leave a mark, a lasting legacy. It is a longing for significance to do something *great* with their lives. But for many Christians, this desire gets distorted and hijacked because they have bought into one of the prevailing myths of our world.

> Making disciples is far more than a program. It is the mission of our lives. It defines us. A disciple is a disciple maker.
>
> —FRANCIS CHAN

The Performance Myth: The best way to make your life count is through personal accomplishments others can see.

The Comfort Myth: Do everything you can to avoid pain and discomfort, and you'll have a great life.

The Generosity Myth: Find the latest and trendiest cause and go all in—show that you are a giver!

The Money Myth: Earn as much as you can . . . save as much as you can . . . a great legacy is all about financial security.

The Pleasure Myth: You only live once, so live it up . . . make that bucket list and do it all.

Even though they want to follow Jesus, many Christians have been subtly seduced by these myths. Every now and then, though, we see God expose and shatter these false narratives. He awakens people from their slumber, and they become gloriously disillusioned with the ways of this world with its empty promises and shallow amusements. People begin to suspect that the Christian life could be richer and more meaningful than they've been led to believe.

We think there's a good chance that you're one these people. You want the things that matter most. You want your life to count for the things of God. But what do you do?

> The will of God is not something you add to your life. It's a course you choose. You either line yourself up with the Son of God . . . or you capitulate to the principle which governs the rest of the world.
>
> —ELIZABETH ELLIOT

What is the great pursuit of your life? What story do you want your life to tell? How do you want to be remembered after you're gone? How you answer these questions will control how you will invest the one life you have to live.

We have prayed earnestly for God to persuade every person who picks up this book to give themselves wholeheartedly to the greatest cause on earth—being a disciple of Jesus, who makes disciples. We call it the greatest cause on earth because when God brings history to an end, it's the only cause that will ultimately matter. Everything else will fade to black. Every other movement has an expiration date. The only revolution that has eternal implications is the one Jesus launched. When it's all said and done, the quality of our lives will be measured by these two questions:

1. Was I a disciple of Jesus?
2. Did I help make disciples of Jesus?

Our achievements and our comforts will be long forgotten. Our generous moments will be remembered, but will the cause to which we contributed be the one that ultimately matters in eternity? Our money will have no value. Our pleasures in this world will be gone. The items on our bucket list that have nothing to do with knowing, trusting, following, treasuring, and proclaiming Jesus will look like utter foolishness.

What can make our lives so different is an unwavering commitment to follow Jesus. His life was filled with purpose, mission, and eternal impact. His life was so remarkable because of his unwavering commitment to reaching lost people and making disciples. He poured his life into the mission to redeem humanity and, in the process, he raised up just a few people. Then he commanded them to do the same with others. In so doing, he started a revolution that changed world history.

> You cannot fulfill God's purpose for your life while focusing on your own plans.
>
> —RICK WARREN

The aim of this book is to help you understand what Jesus did and how he did it—and how you can emulate his commitment to reach people and make disciples. This book is not a textbook; it's a *handbook*. Understanding must lead to application. We want you to read this book and *do something* with it. And don't wait until you're finished reading. You can put these principles into practice as you read.

We also want to encourage you to invite others to join you on the journey of becoming a disciple maker. Process the content with other people. Ponder deeply, think out loud, consider the questions throughout each chapter, and test-drive the portions that grab your attention.

All the events that capture today's headlines will one day look like historical footnotes in comparison to Jesus' grand cause. What we have to show for our lives when we die may not look like much now. But if we lived as disciples who made disciples, what we have built will go on forever. It will make an eternal difference; it will leave an indelible mark, the longest-lasting legacy.

God cares about those around you, including your family, neighbors, friends (both outside and inside church), and coworkers. You have an opportunity to join him in his mission for them. Here are some of the people in whose lives you can make a BIG DIFFERENCE:

- Your children
- Your nonbelieving friends
- Your believing friends
- Your neighbors
- The people where you work
- The people in your church
- The people in your small group or missional community
- The people in your Sunday school class

Watch what Jesus did. He engaged Peter and asked him to follow. The same was true with John, James, and Andrew. He moved toward people. He loved them with a full heart. If you want to see people transformed and redeemed, follow Jesus and do what Jesus did.

In the journey that follows, we are going to paint a picture of how you can create the greatest possible legacy. You will store up treasures in heaven by faithfully following Jesus as your own personal life commitment (we want to first BE what we want others to be), and then you will help other people with their greatest need, which is to learn how to trust and follow Jesus. In the process, we are going to show you some key tools:

- A simple, clear picture of what it means to be a disciple and make disciples
- A practical model for disciple making that you could use right away
- The seven elements of disciple making taken from the life of Jesus
- Inspiration and real-life stories to help you apply these teachings
- An explicit invitation to join the discipleship-first revolution
- An appendix with key insights for pastors and leaders

We will show you how to form your life around Jesus (be a disciple) and how to give the greatest possible gift anyone could ever receive, which is helping people to know Jesus on a deep and personal level—and to participate in his movement (making disciples) with great passion and purpose.

If you are bored and find yourself reaching for something deeper and richer than attending church services or listening to podcasts or sitting through classes, you can give yourself permission to stop consuming religious goods and services that won't equip you to make disciples. We were created for more than this. Jesus invites you to get out of the boat and walk with him into the exhilarating and often unpredictable waters of disciple making.

This is the opportunity of a lifetime. The time for making your life count begins now! Oh, the place he wants to take us!

> You can do more with 12 disciples than with 1,200 religious consumers.
>
> —ALAN HIRSCH

PART 1

MAKE DISCIPLES

Chapter 1

ONE BIG REASON AND SEVEN OTHERS

> "As the Father has sent me, I am sending you."
> JOHN 20:21

> God has raised this Jesus to life, and
> we are all witnesses of it.
> ACTS 2:32

In the spring of 1985, the leadership of Coca-Cola took a big risk.

At the time, the company was steadily losing ground to Pepsi, which had captivated American soda drinkers with its sweet taste and catchy advertising. So Coca-Cola went back to the drawing board and brought in a consultant who encouraged them to reconsider what was core to their mission as a company. He drew a box on a white board and then asked the executives to put one word in the box—a word that encapsulated what Coca-Cola was all about. The overwhelming response was the single word *taste*.

So the folks at Coca-Cola immediately began concocting new formulas and conducting blind taste tests. They settled on a new soft-drink flavor that they believed would win back their old customers and overpower Pepsi. *But that's not what happened.* Maybe you've heard of the product—New Coke. The American public's reaction to the change was very negative, even hostile. People wrote hateful letters. They began stockpiling *old* Coke in fear that it was going away forever. Two weeks after the company launched "New Coke," the leaders of Coca-Cola began to panic.

> All who are called to salvation are called to discipleship, no exceptions, no excuses!
>
> —BILL HULL

It was painfully obvious that this experiment with taste was a major marketing failure, so the leadership of Coca-Cola (minus the consultant) regathered in the same conference room they had met in before and revisited that conversation about the company's identity. They erased the word *taste* and replaced it with a new word—*tradition*. They went back to the company's beginning and came up with a new product based on something very old. This led to the launch of "Coca-Cola Classic." Sales skyrocketed, and Pepsi was no longer a real competitor. The company returned to its roots and reclaimed its story.[1]

It's easy for us to think that we can suddenly change our story, but the truth is far more complicated. People can't just reinvent themselves. We all have a history—a backstory that shapes who we are and where we have come from. The story of Coca-Cola is a reminder to all of us that we come from somewhere. Take a look at your life and the lives of everyday Christians around you. What word goes in your box? What is the core essence of your story? What drives you as you live your life?

We believe that only one word truly belongs in that box: *Jesus*.

Before it became an organized religion, the Christian faith was a movement about *Jesus*. Christianity, at its heart, is not a set of ethical teachings, although Jesus frequently taught people how to live well. Fundamentally, it's not about attending church services or practicing spiritual disciplines, though if you trust and follow Jesus, you'll want to adopt his way of life. The Christian faith didn't begin in a church building or a Bible class. It was born in the hearts of people who placed their faith and trust in a man who walked out of an empty tomb one Sunday morning two millennia ago.

These were people who said they actually saw Jesus, touched him, and ate with him after he rose from the dead. They never claimed to be Bible scholars or experts in theology. They believed that Jesus was the center and source of life. They were disciples of Jesus and they, in turn, made other disciples of Jesus. The claims they made and the things they taught are either right or they're wrong. It's our hope you believe they were telling the truth. We certainly do.

Our lives have been forever changed by those who helped us to trust and follow Jesus. In his youth, Josh was discipled by his grandmother. For Bobby, it was later in life—a French professor on a state college campus. Over the years, we have found our situations, our stories of discipleship, to be similar to the stories of others who are now disciple makers. We've learned that the people most likely to disciple other people *were first discipled themselves*, like we were.

One of the great myths in our day is that all religions are pretty much the same . . . that they all say pretty much the same thing. They don't. We affirm that every religion deserves a measure of respect and should be understood on its own terms. And one of the ways in which Christianity is unique and different from other religions is this: *It focuses on a man who proclaimed the in-breaking kingdom of God through transformational teaching, healing people, and delivering people from the bondage of the enemy. Then he was put to death on a cross and three days later rose from the dead for the forgiveness of our sins, never to die again.* Those who believed this man responded to this truth by creating a disciple-making movement. That movement led to what we call the church—a community of people that literally exploded into existence because of the message and resurrection of Jesus.

In the beginning it was all about Jesus—knowing him, trusting him, following him, treasuring him, and proclaiming him. If you were to ask one of those first Christians to identify a single word that captured their purpose for living, their big *why*, it would be *Jesus*. He was everything to them. We call people like this "discipleship-first" people: their identity is completely wrapped up in *being* disciples of Jesus who *make* disciples of Jesus. This book is a primer on how to become the kind of person who puts Jesus at the center, who makes being a disciple and making other disciples their main thing.

Before we go further, we want to clarify the reason why you would want to do this, the *why* that fuels the *what*. There are compelling motivations that have captured us and encourage us to champion the cause of discipleship and disciple making. We pray they will grab your heart too.

ONE BIG REASON

Let's return to the story of Coca-Cola and the importance of accurately defining what goes in that box. The box represents the core mission and purpose that defines the identity of the company, that one thing that gives meaning to everything else.

We believe that every Christian needs to clearly define what goes in the box at the center of their life, and every local church needs to clarify what goes in the box that defines who they are as a church. We say that we want to honor Jesus and put him at the center of our lives, and we want to help other people to do the same. But *why* do we say that?

Jesus alone is worthy of being the most important thing in our lives—and this truth is at the core of every discipleship lifestyle. Don't miss this! This may sound odd, since this is a book on discipleship, but hear us clearly: The main thing, the ultimate focus of our lives, should not be "discipleship"—that's secondary. The main thing is Jesus—and it is because of who Jesus is and what he said and did that discipleship and disciple making are our driving passion.

To help us see how Jesus forms the core of all disciple making, let's look at two aspects of who Jesus is that define his relationship to us. Christian believers will often describe Jesus as both *Savior* and *Lord*.

Jesus is Savior. First Timothy 2:3–4 tells us that God wants all people to be saved and to come to a knowledge of the truth. That is why he sent Jesus. Whoever believes in Jesus will not perish but have eternal life

(John 3:16). Yet whoever rejects the Son will not see life, for God's wrath remains on that person (John 3:36). When we say that Jesus is our Savior, we are acknowledging that he has "saved" us from something. What do we need to be saved from? He has saved us from experiencing God's wrath and eternal judgment against our rebellion and disobedience to God. Jesus saves us from the eternal consequences of our sin as a sacrifice of atonement for us through his death on the cross (Rom. 3:25). Someone who believes in Jesus is a disciple.

> Does the Gospel I preach and teach have a natural tendency to cause people who hear it to become full-time students of Jesus? Would those who believe it become his apprentices as a natural "next step"? What can we responsibly expect would result from people actually believing the substance of my message?
>
> —DALLAS WILLARD

Jesus saves us from eternal separation from God. But he saves us from more than that. Jesus saves us from Satan, a life of misdirection, a life of confusion, and a life without purpose. Those who trust him as Savior trust him as Savior for all of life—not just for his atoning sacrifice, but also for his teaching, his direction, his example. Jesus saves us from misguided and wasted lives. This is what disciple making is all about.

And that's just the beginning. The implications of salvation are endless. Jesus not only saved us *from* eternal consequences. He saved us *for* something as well. Now that we are at peace with God as a result of Jesus' finished work on the cross, we can step into the kingdom of God—here and now. The kingdom of God was Jesus' favorite topic to talk about. It's an easily misunderstood phrase. So what is it? Put simply, the kingdom of God is a realm where God's rule and authority are unchallenged and freely accepted. It is present wherever God's will is done. The kingdom of God is not far off but is immediately and directly accessible to us through Jesus. By removing the obstacles that blocked us from having fellowship with the Father, Jesus has recruited us to join him in his ongoing work of announcing the kingdom through bold proclamation. He also empowers us with the Holy Spirit so we can demonstrate the reality and power of the kingdom through various good works.

We were saved for citizenship in the unshakable kingdom of God. We have been "rescued from the dominion of darkness and brought into the kingdom" (Col. 1:13).

Jesus is Lord. Romans 14:8 tells us how to focus our lives. Paul says, "If we live, we live for the Lord; and if we die, we die for the Lord. So, whether we live or die, we belong to the Lord." One of our favorite verses is Galatians 2:20. No verse better than this one describes a focus that calls us to be disciples and make disciples.

I have been crucified with Christ and I no longer live, but Christ lives in me. The life I now live in the body, I live by faith in the Son of God, who loved me and gave himself for me.

Being saved by a Savior is wonderful, but it doesn't stop there. Salvation is transformational, changing our foundation—our identity. The Bible says that we must look at our lives (before Christ) as being dead to ourselves but that now we are alive to Jesus. We have a new life, a new identity, and a new calling. With our baptism, we are dead to ourselves (Rom. 6:1–6). We want Jesus to live in us and with us. Jesus is not just our Savior. Jesus is our Lord, our leader, and the one who determines the direction of our life (Acts 2:36). What could be more important than living for the One who not only saved you from the horrifying consequences of sin, but is also the reigning Lord of the universe who gives ultimate meaning to our lives? We give our lives to Jesus as Lord, and we help others to do the same. That is the heart of disciple making.

These passages draw us to discipleship

and disciple making because they are the only appropriate responses to who Jesus is and what he has done for us. We put Jesus in the box because he is the core—the essence of our identity, our mission, and the focus of our lives. He is the only worthy center for a human life. We are so grateful to know him. We want others to know him as we know him. That is why we are disciples who make disciples.

Jesus is our Big Reason!

> The greatest issue facing the world today, with all its heartbreaking needs, is whether those who, by profession or culture, are identified as "Christians" will become disciples—students, apprentices, practitioners—of Jesus Christ, steadily learning from him.
>
> —DALLAS WILLARD

Discipleship and disciple making are simply forming our lives around Jesus and helping others to do the same.

THE SEVEN OTHER RELATED REASONS . . .

There are seven other related reasons that compel us to be disciples who make disciples. In addition to putting Jesus in his rightful place in our lives and helping others to do the same, we hope that you will find these biblical reasons for making disciples compelling as well. When we personally make disciples, we engage in the most important mission in life.

1. We obey Jesus' final command.

The last thing Jesus said during his earthly ministry was "go and make disciples" (Matt. 28:19–20). Notice the clarity and directness of Jesus' words. There's only one intellectually respectable way to interpret this statement: "Do with others what I've been doing with you." We either do it or we don't. He's either our Lord or he isn't.

We don't want to overemphasize this, but it needs to be said. If you were to summarize Jesus' teachings, you would find that Jesus not only commanded discipleship in general, but also commanded a specific kind of discipleship. We call it *intentional relational discipleship*. In other words, Jesus didn't just give his disciples a command and abandon them. No, he taught them and showed them how to raise up intentional followers (Luke 10:1–12). He taught his disciples the kind of life required of a disciple, one marked by the supremacy of *agape love* (John 13:34–35). And then he commissioned his disciples (and us by extension) to go and make disciples.

In Luke 6:40, Jesus described it this way: "The student is not above the teacher, but everyone who is fully trained will be like their teacher." In his Great Commission to make disciples, Jesus assumed that his disciples would do for others what Jesus had done for them. And in light of that, he commanded: "Go and make disciples of all nations, baptizing them in the name of the Father and of the Son and of the Holy Spirit" (Matt. 28:19). Making disciples as Jesus made disciples was the operating assumption of the very first Christians. It was nonnegotiable; we must obey our Lord.

2. We follow Jesus.

We want to be like Jesus, and he is the ultimate disciple maker. Consider this—Jesus is the most brilliant and wise person who has ever walked the earth. He was also the most loving. And in light of that, he chose to devote himself to intentionally pouring his time and energy into a few people. He knew something we often miss. God does his most exquisite work in small ways. He brought his teaching and his power to bear on a small group. Remember that this was no mere man! This was God in the flesh! And yet what was his method? If you want to know God's will, take a look at Jesus (John 1:18). Yes, Jesus adapted his approach to the first-century culture. Yes, Jesus adopted the practices of many rabbis and philosophers of his day. But his method was also unique, revealing his wisdom and understanding of people.

Jesus began his ministry by establishing a group of people to invest in. One of his first acts was to form his small group (Matt. 4:18–22; Luke 6:13), and then he trained various-sized groups of people: the seventy-two (Luke 10:1), the Twelve (Matt. 10:2–4), and the inner three (Matt. 17:1). The eternal Son of God didn't need the companionship or assistance of the apostles. Yet from the very beginning, he *chose* to establish and minister within a framework of relationships.

> Jesus poured His life into a few disciples and taught them to make other disciples. Seventeen times we find Jesus with the masses, but forty-six times we see Him with His disciples.
>
> —DANN SPADER

Jesus spent the vast majority of his time with just a few people. If you add up the amount of time Jesus spent with the apostles, you would find that this group consumed most of his time and energy. Bill Hull has estimated that Jesus spent up to 90 percent of his time with the Twelve.[2] They were together constantly. They traveled together, shared meals, experienced mutual hardship, and lived together day after day. As Jesus' crucifixion and death drew closer, he spent even more time with his small group and less time with the great crowds that sought him out. Evidently, Jesus believed that investing his time in a few people was the most strategic investment of his few years on earth.

The Bible tells us that "in Christ all the fullness of the Deity lives in bodily form" (Col. 2:9) and in him "are hidden all the treasures of wisdom and knowledge" (Col. 2:3). The principles he utilized are worth imitating. They are as transcultural as they are transformative, effective among all people groups, in all places, and at all times.

3. We help people receive eternal life.

The Bible tells us that God is the initiator and author of our faith (John 6:65; 16:7–11; Acts 7:51; Heb. 12:2). At the same time, the Bible tells us that no one can believe unless they hear the Word of God. And Paul tells us how God does this: faith comes from hearing a message, and that message is heard through the preaching of the word about Christ, the gospel (Rom. 10:17). For the gospel to be preached, Paul tells us that God uses *people* as the conduit for other people to hear the Word of God:

How, then, can they call on the one they have not believed in? And how can they believe in the one of whom they have not heard? And how can they hear without someone preaching to them? (Rom. 10:14)

The preaching described here is not just the message you hear on a Sunday morning or from a street corner evangelist. It's any communication of the good news about Jesus, who he is and what he has done. It can be someone who simply shares the good news of what God has done for us in Jesus in a conversation with a neighbor or a friend over coffee. This kind of "proclaiming" (the meaning of the word *preaching*) happens in countless contexts. Let me (Bobby) share how this happened in my own life.

I was a student at the University of Calgary in Canada when I first made a life-changing decision that I would personally trust and follow Jesus. But before I made that decision, there was a process of investigating the truth. I had lots of questions. What if it was all just a myth? What if the Bible was not accurately preserved? How could I know? Who could I trust?

I learned that my French professor was a Christian, so after talking with him after class one day, I invited him to tell me about his faith and asked him to help me with my questions. He not only started answering my questions, he invited me to join him in an ongoing conversation, meeting regularly. It was more than just talking. He became a friend, a model for me of what a real Christian looks like. What he did for me is what we call "discipling someone."

My professor moved from being "Dr. Jacobs" to being "Mac." He moved from being my French professor to being a friend, then a friend to my family, then my personal life coach and mentor. Mac taught me about Jesus, and we talked about the Bible. Mac not only helped me to "hear the message," but to believe it, understand it, receive it, and then live it out. And he did the same for my parents.

Mac didn't just tell me a few facts about Jesus and then baptize me. He committed to a real life-on-life relationship with me, and he showed me by his own example what it meant to trust and follow Jesus. He was there on the day I got married and on many other days when the direction of my life was set by God. I can never thank him enough for his willingness to be used by God as a disciple who makes disciples.

4. We give people the personal help they need.

People aren't born knowing how to embrace Jesus as Savior and follow him as Lord. Someone has to tell them about him and show them what it looks like to turn their lives over to him. Much has been said and written about how many self-proclaimed Christians live and talk and think like unbelievers. And we need to be honest—too many churchgoers are *not* Jesus-followers.

Many things that happen in a church do not lead to changed lives. Preaching plays an important role in communicating God's Word, but sermons *alone* are unlikely to change people in deep and lasting ways. Big events and programs can be encouraging and even inspiring, but people need ways to slow down and focus on the deeper things of life and relational growth. Church leaders across the land are quickly realizing that something more transformative is needed than an outreach event. It's not difficult to convince a pastor or church leader that discipleship is the answer—but few know what to do about it.

Jesus' method of disciple making doesn't work at a surface level. It compels us to connect with people in a deeply personal way. It's life on life, up front and in your face. It's motivated by love, fueled by the Holy Spirit, and the end result is dramatic transformation. Making disciples of Jesus means helping people learn and understand and take steps to trust and follow Jesus in the real world, not just having theoretical discussions in a classroom. And the real world is where people's lives are complex, busy, and confusing—even overwhelming.

Jesus' method teaches us that disciples are hand-crafted, one life at a time, not mass-produced in a religious factory.

The sad truth is that most people do not realize how much they *need* to be discipled. I (Josh) still remember when I first experienced this realization. It was the last day of the spring semester of my freshman year of college, and I was packing my bag and preparing to go home. My friends had already left campus, and I had just said good-bye to my girlfriend (who would eventually become my wife). And suddenly, I felt alone and afraid. Going home meant facing the pain of my broken family.

My mom was an addict, enslaved to alcohol and prescription drugs. I knew that my nine-year-old brother would be depending on me during the summer to be there for him, to help raise him. And I also had to work to pay for college. The pressure was too much for me. I sensed I was in over my head, and I felt the weight of the world crushing me down. All I could do was drop to my knees and cry out to God. Though I had been baptized as a Christian five years earlier, I had no idea how to live as a follower of Jesus. I had never experienced the power of Jesus or appreciated the wisdom of Jesus. My church attendance record was nearly perfect, but my faith was weak and undeveloped. I had more than a decade of Christian education

under my belt, but I had no clue how to apply what I already knew. I needed someone to meet me where I was and make an intentional effort to invest in my spiritual maturity.

God answered my cry of need and despair, and he sent several people into my life to disciple and mentor me. Today, he's sending me back out, into the lives of others. That's how it works.

5. We change lives.

We know Jesus is alive today. The Bible tells us that he was raised from the dead and will one day return to bring his kingdom rule to fulfillment here on earth. And one of the main reasons we know—experientially—that Jesus is alive is that he is still changing lives. People still encounter him today. Every century, every continent, every culture—rich, poor, young, old, well-educated, illiterate, beaten, broken, arrogant, afraid—all kinds of people are forever transformed when they see Jesus for who he really is.

> People who are addicted say, "I met him, and Jesus set me free."
> People who are alone say, "He found me in a dark place, and I'm not alone anymore."
> People who are hopeless say, "I was about to give up, and now I have hope."
> People who are bitter say, "I was living

in a prison of resentment, and now I know what it means to forgive."

People who are anxious say, "I was constantly worried, and Jesus gave me peace."

People who are self-righteous say, "I was caught up in pride, and Jesus showed me the way of grace."

People who are discouraged say, "I was down and out, but Jesus picked me up."

People who are desperate say, "I was at the end of my rope, and Jesus found me there."

PAUSE AND PONDER

Look back on your life and think of specific moments when Jesus met you in a hard or painful place. How did he help you?

I (Josh) know a young man named Mark who was on the brink of self-destruction. He partied away his first semester of junior college and was later kicked out of school. He was devastated by his loss and ashamed of his behavior. Soon afterward he came home one day, went upstairs to his room, closed the door, and laid face down on the floor, sobbing, praying, and lamenting what he had done. When he finally got up from the floor, he reached for a Bible and turned to Ephesians 2. He will tell you that as he read the first ten verses of Ephesian 2, something supernatural happened to him. He fell into a deep sleep that night and awoke the next morning to a sense of peace that he'd never known before.

Over the next few hours, Mark set out on a trajectory of redemption. He broke up with his girlfriend because he knew in his heart that their relationship was impure. He gave away his expensive designer clothes because he felt too attached to his wardrobe. He went to work that day and shared what was happening to him with his boss, a man named Collin, who was a bi-vocational pastor and a committed disciple maker. God forged an unbreakable bond between these two men, and over the next three years, Collin spent a lot of time with Mark, encouraging him, listening to him, correcting him, reassuring him, calling out good in him. He helped Mark discover his spiritual gifts, and in a three-year period Mark went from an unbeliever to a disciple maker himself, investing in the lives of others. This is the handiwork of Jesus!

6. We truly love others!

The Bible tells us that God is love. God loves us and fills our hearts with love for others (Rom. 5:5; 1 John 4:19). Loving God and loving people is the passion behind all disciple making—the motive behind the mission, the heart behind the hands. We reach out to our neighbors, we serve others, and we disciple people because we *love* them. We feel compelled to reach out and to make disciples of lost people because they are eternally lost (2 Thess. 1:8–10), and we want them to know the Savior. We want people to have the treasure of living every day for Jesus as Lord (Col. 2:2–3). We reach out to immature Christians or non-discipled Christians because we love them and we want them to become the people God wants them to become. As Dann Spader says, "Love is the signature card of true disciples. Disciple making cannot happen apart from loving, caring relationships—both tough and a tender love" (see 1 Thess. 2).[3]

As I (Bobby) was finishing my seminary degree, I completed an independent study where I created a biblical theology—a summary of the top teaching of the New Testament. And what did I learn? *Agape love* came out as the single most important virtue in the New Testament—the one held up above all others. In 1 Corinthians 13, Paul says that love is more important than experiences of the Spirit, than knowledge, even than serving the poor (vv. 1–3). Without love, we gain nothing. Paul says three things will remain: faith, hope, and love—but the greatest is love. And Jesus said that it is by our love that all men will know

that we are true disciples (John 13:34–35). *Agape love* is the trademark stamped on every authentic follower of Jesus.

After completing my study project, I realized I had a problem. When I talked about the central importance of love at churches with people I knew, most of them were not quite sure what to do about it. Most of their time was focused on more pragmatic concerns, things like running weekly programs or choosing music or teaching a class. And while there is nothing wrong with any of these things, most churches today are primarily focused on running gatherings and programs. We should know—we are both pastors! Even the lives of individual Christians are often so busy with attending church services and programs that they don't have much room for connecting relationally with people. Our models of church and Christian living in America today are not formed around relationships where we grow to love and care for other people.

I was faced with a dilemma. The churches all around me, including my own church, were not set up to develop relationships and model Jesus-like love to one another. I knew I had to pursue a different way of doing church, but it would take me more than a few years to understand how to do it—and I'm still learning.[4]

Jesus' style of disciple making makes love

our primary motivation and focus. Love is the foundation of disciple making from the time someone first hears about Jesus through his or her conversion, early spiritual growth, and up through the time when that person becomes a disciple maker too. If we model what we do after Jesus, *agape love* becomes the motivation, the environment in which our discipleship happens, and the fruit of our discipleship efforts.[5]

PAUSE AND PONDER

Who has stepped into your life and loved you well? How did they demonstrate their love for you?

---

7. We live out the ministry of all believers.

You (yes, you!) can be a disciple who makes disciples. God calls us to be ministers (Rom. 12:3–8). We talk to people all the time who feel spiritually inadequate or ill-equipped to make disciples of Jesus. They assume that disciple making is something for pastors or "professional" Christians. But if the ministry of Jesus and the message of the Epistles teach us anything, it's that anybody—no matter who they are—can become a disciple maker. Envision some of the people we know (not their real names).

Jim is a general contractor in the church we

serve. Jesus rescued him from the bondage of drug addiction a few years ago. He and his wife were on the brink of divorce, but at just the right time, Jesus scooped them up and turned their tragedy of destruction into a story of miraculous reconciliation. Now he leverages his influence on the job site and in other venues to help men to trust and follow Jesus.

Crystal is a stay-at-home mom who has a burden for the moms in her neighborhood who may not know Jesus. She and her husband, Scott, walk down the same streets every day—praying for God to open doors and give them favor with their neighbors. She is currently cultivating spiritual friendships with twelve different women who live near her, and she hosts a weekly discipleship group in her home.

Robert is a professor of music at a local university. Before he began his teaching career, he performed with a world-renowned philharmonic orchestra. He views himself as a secret agent of the kingdom of God as he invests in college students from all over the world. At the risk of losing his job, he regularly prays with students and shares Jesus stories with them when he feels prompted by God to do so. He invites the students who are open to Christ into a group where they explore the Scriptures together and share their lives with one another.

Sarah is a bookkeeper for a nonprofit

Chapter 2

THE GREATEST CAUSE ON EARTH

"Therefore go and make disciples of all nations."
MATTHEW 28:19

We hope the vision of a Jesus-centered life of being a disciple and making disciples has captured you the way it has captured us. In this chapter, we want to dig a little deeper into the call to make disciples, and we'd like to start out with two quizzes.

Don't worry, these won't go on your transcript. They will help you better understand how you can apply the things we learned in the last chapter to your life today.[1]

- Name the five wealthiest people in the country.
- Name the last five Heisman trophy winners.

- Name five people who have won a Nobel or Pulitzer prize.
- Name five athletes who won gold medals.
- Name five Academy Award winners.

How did you do?

We didn't do very well either. Yet these are the prominent people in the headlines and on television. They seem so important and successful. But to whom? The names are popular for a moment and then easily forgotten. Several years ago I (Bobby) remember wandering into a cemetery in Princeton, New Jersey, and walking around, looking at the tombstones of wealthy and famous people. It rocked me to see how dilapidated the tombstones and the area around them had become. Nothing but crumbling rocks among weeds. "These were famous people," I said to myself, "and this is all that is left?"

Okay, now for quiz number two.

- Name five people who have made a difference in your life.
- Name five people who have loved you and supported you.
- Name five people who have helped you in a difficult time.
- Name five people who have helped you in your spiritual journey.
- Name the people who helped you commit your life to Christ.

Isn't that a much easier test? It was for us too.

And what does this teach us? *That people who make the biggest difference in our lives are not famous. They are everyday people who care about us and demonstrate their love for us.* It's those everyday, ordinary people who are most likely to help us on our spiritual journey.

This demonstrates the truth we saw earlier that disciples of Jesus are not mass-produced, but handcrafted, one person at a time. And that's the work of everyday disciples who make disciples. We want you to become THAT kind of person!

But you probably need some help to get there. We all do.

You are not alone. Most everyday Christians do not know how to make disciples. We know because we've talked with them. They tell us, "I have never been discipled, so I do not know how to disciple others," or "I need someone to show me how to do it!" In fact, in our experience, the vast majority of Christians would say the same thing. And it makes sense: *How can you do for others what you have never been equipped to do yourself?* So how do you do it? We have written this book to help answer that question. But before we jump in, we want to give you some additional background on ourselves as well as some key definitions that you will need to keep in your mind throughout the book.

ABOUT THE AUTHORS, BOBBY AND JOSH

Who are we? We serve together in ministry at Harpeth Christian Church in Franklin, Tennessee (just outside Nashville), and we really enjoy working together to disciple people and train disciple makers. We have different backgrounds (Bobby grew up in Canada; Josh is from Alabama) and personalities (Bobby is a get-it-done entrepreneurial leader who loves to teach the Bible; Josh is a passionate, extroverted shepherd-preacher).

We have written this handbook because we believe that you, like the rest of us, need help. In this book we will share with you the seven principles of a discipleship lifestyle. These are principles by which we seek to live out a life with Jesus at the center, making disciples. We don't have it all together by any stretch of the imagination. Every single day, we feel like kindergartners in Jesus' school of discipleship. But we were privileged to experience being discipled by others.

Bobby is the lead and founding pastor of our church and is now in his late fifties. Josh is the teaching and discipleship minister and is in his late thirties. Although we were discipled, we have also learned many of the lessons we share in this book the hard way—through trial and failure. But we are tenacious. After stumbling, praying, and living through the school of hard knocks, we have learned a few things we think are worth sharing.

For example, we both have found that the most difficult part of disciple making is usually *making time for relationships*. We talk relationships, teach relationships, preach relationships, and tell others to focus on relationships. But it's so easy to get busy and forget to actually invest in relationships and give ourselves to them the way we would like. Or we overestimate our capacities, and we have too many relationships, and we can't handle them all well. We also want to pray more than we do. The list could go on, but we share this much to let you know that we don't have it down perfect. We hope that some of the things we are still learning will be helpful to you as we let you know how we are growing.

> God has not promised to bless our good motives, dreams, and innovation. He has promised to bless his plan; that plan is that disciples make other disciples—everything else is a sideshow.
>
> —BILL HULL

In the last chapter, Bobby described being discipled by his French professor at the University of Calgary. My story (Josh) is a little different. I attended church every week for most of my childhood, and my grandmother was my primary spiritual influence. I was blessed to have many remarkable Christians who showed up in my life at just the right time to teach me to trust and follow Jesus, but even with these helpful influences in my life, it wasn't until my sophomore year of college that I really began to take the message of Jesus seriously for my own life.

In more recent years, I've been "discipled" by a battle with cancer. I never would've asked for such a scary ordeal, but as I've struggled with questions about God and the way he works in the life of a believer, I've seen Jesus use this pain and suffering to show what it means to trust him. As strange as it might sound, I am genuinely grateful for this trial. Jesus has never been more real and alive to me than he is right now. And I'm certain that God is using cancer to make me a better man. I work on staff at our church with Bobby, and in addition to sharing preaching responsibilities with him, I write the discipleship curriculum for the church, coach small group leaders, and help people tap into the transforming power of Jesus in their everyday lives.

We think we are both ridiculously blessed. We get to spend our lives heralding the world's most inspiring message (Jesus) and equipping people to participate in the greatest cause on earth (disciple making)! We have also been privileged to learn from other disciple makers. We are involved with a ministry called **discipleship .org,** a network of disciple-making leaders from around the world. Bobby leads this ministry and coordinates national and regional gatherings called Disciple-Making Forums. We both get a front-row seat to learn some of the proven principles that can make the biggest difference in effectively training and multiplying disciples, and we want to share these principles with you.

> The world can no longer be left to mere diplomats, politicians, and business leaders. They have done the best they could, no doubt. But this is an age for spiritual heroes—a time for men and women to be heroic in their faith and in spiritual character and power.
>
> —DALLAS WILLARD

We believe that *any* person who loves and follows Jesus can become a disciple maker, even if they were not personally discipled themselves. What's most important is looking closely at the life of Jesus, taking his words to heart, and then seeking to replicate Jesus' life-on-life method in your own context. It's all grounded in relationships, intentional guidance, and coaching, and it leads people to become more like Jesus.

DEFINITIONS

Before we jump into the characteristics of a disciple-making life, it's essential that you know what we are talking about. People sometimes use the same words, but they can mean very different things. And that eventually leads to problems. So while some of you might find this next part boring, we'd ask that you stick with us and pay attention to these key definitions because they are foundational. If we can agree on what these words mean, it will make the more practical parts in later chapters easier to follow.

Definitions are important because when words are used correctly, they describe reality. Having clear definitions and realistic goals makes it much easier to engage in disciple making and find success in what you do. We have five specific definitions that we have found are foundational to the effective use of this manual. We define what it is to be a *disciple* and what we mean when we talk about *disciple making*. We also want you to know *who we are talking about* when we talk about discipling people, and what we mean when we talk about *Jesus' method* of disciple making. Lastly, we want to outline *the seven elements of Jesus' philosophy* described in this book, called *intentional relational discipleship*.

We won't claim that our definitions are inspired by God. They aren't verbatim from the Bible either. But they are based on what the Bible teaches. And they are real-world tested, simple and clear, and usable for everyday disciple makers.

1. DISCIPLE

Disciple makers have an end goal—making disciples! And the definition of a disciple can be formed around the words of Jesus in Matthew 4:19. This passage is easy to reference and memorize:[2]

> And he said to them, "Follow me, and I will make you fishers of men" (ESV).

We like this verse because it can be divided easily into a three-part framework that matches the three key aspects of discipleship that we find in the rest of the New Testament. What are the three aspects that define a disciple?

1. "Following" Jesus (head)
2. "Being changed" by Jesus through the Holy Spirit (heart)
3. Being committed to the mission of Jesus, which is to be "fishers of men" (hands)

Putting all three together, we arrive at the following definition of a disciple:

A disciple is someone who is following Jesus, being changed by Jesus, and is committed to the mission of Jesus.

We want you to make disciples who fit this description. If people are *following* Jesus, being *changed* by Jesus, and are *committed* to the *mission* of Jesus, then they are biblical disciples, as we understand it. And if our goal is to make disciples, it is vitally important to define success and to know what it looks like when our mission is accomplished.

PAUSE AND PONDER

Why is it important to be clear about a biblical definition of a disciple?

---

2. DISCIPLE MAKING

We now know what a disciple is. But what is meant by the expression *disciple making*?[3] We believe Matthew 28:18–20 gives us the best foundation for understanding and defining Jesus' mandate to make disciples:

> Then Jesus came to them and said, "All authority in heaven and on earth has been given to me. Therefore go and make disciples of all nations, baptizing them in the name of the Father and of the Son and of the Holy Spirit, and teaching them to obey everything I have

commanded you. And surely I am with you always, to the very end of the age."

In the original Greek text, there is only one imperative command in this verse: we are to *make disciples*.[4] This command is followed by what are called participial phrases, three of them, which describe *how* we make disciples: we go, we baptize, and we teach obedience. We use the three parts of this key text to keep our definition of disciple making theologically tight and easily applicable.

> We have too many Christians who have accepted Jesus into their hearts and who have been baptized and who have confessed their sins and who have joined the Church and who are in Bible studies and who are absolutely 100 percent convinced they are going to heaven, but who are not followers of Jesus.
>
> —SCOT MCKNIGHT

1. *Helping People*—This is how we apply the "go" part of the command (v. 19). The expression "helping people" communicates how we "go," that we do this in a warm, relational manner, as modeled by Jesus. When we go into the world, we enter into the lives of others as Jesus did to "help" them find salvation and learn how to live the kingdom life as a follower of Jesus.

2. *Trust*—This is how we apply the "baptize" part of the command. One's decision to trust in Jesus, according to the text, is expressed by baptism "in the name of the Father and of the Son and of the Holy Spirit" (v. 19). The act of baptism communicates our trust in Jesus and is at the root of repentance and conversion. Trust and faith lie at the heart of the entire Christian life. Trust is also Trinitarian: we trust Jesus in the power of the Spirit to the glory of God the Father.

3. *Follow*—This is how we apply the "obey everything I have commanded you" part of the command (v. 20). Disciple making leads to obedience and sanctification (the process of being progressively transformed by the Spirit into the image of Jesus). And it naturally includes and leads to the command to make other disciples (mission is built into the process).

4. *Jesus*—Though it is not one of the three parts of the command, we want to reemphasize that Jesus is the one we focus on as we "make disciples" (vv. 19–20). He is the object and center in discipleship; disciples are to become his "apprentices" and "live life" as he would live.

With these four components from Matthew 28 in mind, we define disciple making this way:

Disciple making is helping people to trust and follow Jesus.

This is a simple definition, but not a simplistic one.

> The church exists for nothing else but to draw men into Christ, to make them little Christs. If they are not doing that, all the cathedrals, clergy, missions, sermons, even the Bible itself, are simply a waste of time. God became man for no other purpose.
>
> —C. S. LEWIS

We have found this definition to be surprisingly usable and sticky in our local church context, where adults, high school students, and children easily adopt it as their common way to express their involvement in disciple making. It encompasses all of the teachings of the Bible, telling us to just rely on God—his grace, his promises, and his power. And it encompasses all the teachings in the Bible where we must act—obedience, faithfulness, and resisting sin. Both parts are essential to balanced discipleship.[5] This statement is the mission statement of our local church, plastered on the back wall of our sanctuary and on all our important documents. We will use this definition as the foundation for this book as we unpack the seven elements of the discipleship lifestyle.

This definition, like the one we gave earlier

for a disciple, is not Scripture. But we have found it to be very useful and helpful in following what is taught in Scripture. Your church or your leaders may use different definitions than the ones we've given here. That's okay! We may use different words or phrase things a bit differently, but the important thing is that our definitions reflect what the Bible teaches, they are clear, and they are something we can remember. We won't quibble with the specific words you choose to use as long as your definitions help you to truly follow God in being a disciple and making disciples.

PAUSE AND PONDER

Can you think of other church or religious definitions that you use every day? What do you mean when you say someone is a "Christian," or someone is "saved," or someone "attends church with me"? Why are definitions important for effectiveness?

---

3. DISCIPLE MAKING IS BOTH EVANGELISM AND DISCIPLESHIP

Many people are unaware of the fact that the command to *win converts* is found nowhere in the Bible. You might want to think about that for a minute (and check your Bible). The Bible doesn't teach us to make converts because the teaching about disciple making applies to *both* non-Christians and Christians. Sometimes people refer to discipling non-Christians as evangelism. We won't take issue with that, but we find it easier and more biblical to think of disciple making as something we do for both non-Christians and Christians.[6] Making disciples isn't just how we learn to be a Christian—and then it's over. It begins before our conversion and continues for the rest of our life as a follower of Jesus!

Read the Gospels and you'll find that Jesus was making disciples of Peter, James, and John (and the others among the Twelve) long before they truly believed that he was the Jewish Messiah. In fact, it can be a fun and intriguing exercise to study and try to determine when the disciples were truly converted. Follow the story line of Peter in the gospel of Luke and try to pinpoint the exact moment when he was fully converted. Good luck with that! We'll warn you in advance . . . it's impossible to know for sure.

But that's the point we're trying to make. Rather than focusing on conversion as a clear line we want people to cross, we need something more organic. We need a process that includes more than just conversion, something that helps people apply everything that Jesus commanded to who they are and who they are becoming—now and for all eternity. That's a bigger shift than you may realize. Let's look again at what Jesus says about making disciples in the Great Commission in Matthew 28:19–20:

> "Therefore go and make disciples of all nations, baptizing them in the name of the Father and of the Son and of the Holy Spirit, and *teaching them to obey everything I have commanded you.* And surely I am with you always, to the very end of the age" (emphasis added).

Disciple making is about more than just decisions and baptisms. Too many people think that conversion is the finish line. Once you are in, the work is done—just live a good life until you die or Jesus returns, and God takes care of the rest. Wrong! As wonderful as it is when someone surrenders to Jesus and is baptized, that doesn't mean the job is done. According to Jesus, conversion is the starting line (or pretty close to it).

When we accept salvation, there is a whole life of growing as a disciple of Jesus that lies in front of us. Jesus calls us to follow him, and that's not something we postpone for heaven; it begins here and now. Disciple making is about becoming the kind of people who are *prepared* for heaven, whose loves and desires

and habits are attuned to a world where God is visibly glorified and all of life is about living in God's presence and loving him. So disciple making is about equipping people to embrace the lifestyle of surrender and obedience to *all of Jesus' teachings, here and now.*

> Non-discipleship is the elephant in the church; it is not the many moral failures, financial abuses, or amazing general similarity between Christians and non-Christians. These are only the effects of the underlying problem.
>
> —DALLAS WILLARD

We know that some may push back on what we're saying here. You may even feel like we're advocating a form of works-based righteousness. But that's not at all what we're saying. Jesus said much the same; just look at Matthew 28. It's straight from his mouth. We need to understand that both conversion and discipleship are supernatural occurrences.[7] The Holy Spirit catalyzes and supercharges *both* the new birth and the discipleship process. While we contribute nothing to our justification (our righteous standing and acceptance before God), in the process of growing as a disciple (our sanctification), we enter into a divine partnership with God, the one who ultimately makes all things possible.

So while conversion is the most important step in the journey, involving a fundamental change in our identity, life transformation is the end goal. The mission Jesus entrusted to us is to teach people how to form their entire lives around this new identity, rooted in his lordship. This is why our definition of disciple is not just about the commitment to *follow* Jesus but also to *be changed* by Jesus and *be committed* to his kingdom mission. We want whole life discipleship because we want whole life disciples.

> ══ **PAUSE AND PONDER** ══
>
> Why is it important to make conversion the starting line of salvation rather than the finish line?

4. JESUS' METHOD

Jesus didn't just give us a message, he also gave us a method. We believe he invites us to embrace his method of disciple making. Both his message *and his method* are inspired. They both originate with God. Many books have been written that aim to clarify Jesus' *message*,[8] but in this book we want to also look at his method—not just the "what" but the "how."

While most people will readily agree that discipleship is a good and necessary thing, few understand how to practically apply Jesus' method to discipleship. We want to hold up Jesus' method of disciple making as the best way to live as well as the most fruitful way to build the local church. We think that the best way forward for the church is to return with passion to both aspects of Jesus' ministry.[9] A Jesus-centered church will proclaim *his* message with boldness and love and practice *his* methods with resolve and focus. To this end, we'd encourage you to read and study the Gospels and pay close attention to how Jesus discipled people. What Jesus did is so different from what most church leaders are doing today. Maybe that's the reason so much of what we do seems so ineffective.

Again, we want to emphasize that all of this isn't just for super-Christians or the spiritually or theologically elite. This is something all of us who follow Jesus can do, everyday Christians who love Jesus and want to honor him with their lives.

> ══ **PAUSE AND PONDER** ══
>
> Review the seven motivations for a disciple-making focus from the last chapter. Which of the seven is most personally motivating to you and why?

5. JESUS' METHOD IS INTENTIONAL RELA-TIONAL DISCIPLESHIP

Some of you may be familiar with the name Robert Coleman. If you aren't, we want to introduce you to him. As of this writing, Dr. Robert Coleman is in his late eighties, but though he is growing older, he remains sharp and wise. He is a true Christian gentleman. In the early 1960s, Dr. Coleman wrote a book on disciple making called *The Master Plan of Evangelism*.[10] It has sold more than 3.5 million copies in English and far more in the more than a hundred languages into which it has been translated. It's now considered the gold standard—a modern classic on Jesus' method of disciple making.

We've learned a great deal from Dr. Coleman, both from reading his book and from getting to know him personally over the past few years. One of the unique teachings in his book is his argument that the *method* of discipleship used by Jesus is perfect, the best way of making disciples. Jesus was fully human and fully God, and he himself was perfect, both without sin and infinitely wise. We miss much of the wisdom of Jesus if all we pay attention to are the words he spoke. We must also observe

how he interacted with people, the methods he used to train and teach and communicate with his disciples. We were blessed to work with Dr. Coleman on a new project recently,[11] and in that resource he summarized the "Jesus method" around nine key principles.

> Far too many of us assume that discipleship is merely the transfer of information leading to behavior modification. But discipleship, at heart, involves transformation at the deepest levels of our understanding, affection, and will by the Holy Spirit, through the Word of God, and in relationship with the people of God.
>
> —JIM PUTMAN

We love his summary! But we are pastors, and we also know that while nine principles might work in an academic class, they are too many for the average person to easily remember. In addition, as they are currently written, they do not easily translate to the various spheres of life, contexts like leading a small group or meeting with a group of young marrieds or meeting one-on-one for a coffee to talk about the Bible. We believe Jesus' method applies to *every* sphere of the Christian life from A to Z, so we worked with Dr. Coleman's time-tested, biblical insights and developed a new framework that we hope is easier for you to remember and apply.

We start by defining the method Jesus used to train disciples as *Intentional Relational Discipleship*. Here is what those three words mean:

- **Intentional**—Jesus' example and the Great Commission of Matthew 28 teach us to be guided by intention, planning, and strategic thinking. Intentionality is grounded in being deliberate; it is thoughtfulness in action.
- **Relational**—Jesus' example and the teaching of the New Testament show us that disciple making is relational. "Jesus-style" love (John 13:34–35) for people is both the foundational environment for disciple making and the ultimate fruit of disciple making.[12]
- **Discipleship**—The word *discipleship* describes the *state of being a disciple*. It is often used as a synonym for *disciple making*. We conceive of discipleship as the process of being made into a disciple of Jesus.

These three words could serve as a good summary of Jesus' method, but they still do not tell us enough. So we worked with Dr. Coleman and several other national discipleship leaders[13] to develop seven transferable principles that will help you to fully understand what Jesus would *do* and *how* he might engage in disciple making in your own context. To keep things simple and easy to remember and apply, we used seven one-word elements or statements. For those who learn visually, we have also created icons. And we have definitions for each of the seven—what we call the "elements" of discipleship lifestyle. We hope they make disciple making practical and doable.

Relationships—The central impulse for explaining Jesus' mission to others and to make disciples is love. As John 3:16 says, "For God so loved the world that he gave his one and only Son." By his example, Jesus showed us that disciple making is the development of genuine life-on-life relationships motivated by Jesus-style love.

Jesus—Jesus drew people to himself. He was unabashed and clear in speaking the truth. He is the centerpiece and the focus of all discipleship. We are not discipling people into a program, we are introducing them to a person. The mission of Jesus was to give himself in love for the sake of others so that people would know him, treasure him, and promote him and his message to others.

Intentionality—Jesus had a strategy. He had a plan, a road map for making disciples, what Dr. Robert Coleman calls *The Master Plan.* Jesus guided, coached, and developed his disciples into disciple makers and released them, commissioning them to disciple others as Jesus had discipled them. Their disciple-making work changed the world.

Bible—The Word of God is the training manual that Jesus relied upon in his ministry and provided for all discipleship and teaching. As the author of the Scriptures, Jesus has provided its contents, in both the Old and New Testaments, to give us his teaching, his correction, and his training on the important matters of life and godliness.

Spirit—Jesus' life and ministry were fueled by the Holy Spirit. After living for thirty years in obscurity, Jesus began formally making disciples after the Spirit descended upon him when he was baptized. From that point forward, he remained in a constant state of openness to the Spirit.

Journey—Jesus led his disciples on a journey, inviting them to learn by walking with him and watching him. Though it is a disjointed growth story, it begins with his invitation to come and see and culminates with the Great Commission, where they are sent to go and multiply.

Multiply—Jesus' master plan was to make disciples who were like him in their message and their methods, and then to multiply them by sending them out to disciple others as they had been discipled by him. Jesus teaches us to make disciples who make disciples until the end of time.

These seven elements aren't intended to be the only way you can describe Jesus' method of discipleship. They are simply a framework that we've found helpful in summarizing Jesus' method, a framework that is useful for personal discipleship and for teaching in a local church context. We hope it is useful to you as well. That said, feel free to tweak, adapt, and alter it to fit your own context. The framework is not the goal; it is a tool to accomplish the goal.

PAUSE AND PONDER

Review these seven elements and note which ones make the most sense to you. Which ones do not initially make sense? Why?

YOU'RE INVITED!

We started this chapter asking you to recall the names of people who are commonly considered successful. The rich, athletic, intelligent, and powerful. But we quickly saw that when it comes to individual people, true influence isn't dependent on these things. Real, lasting influence is a matter of relationship. We believe true impact and success are found when we engage in life-on-life relationships with other people. When the story of human history has been written, we believe the unsung work of disciple making will be at the heart of it all. The work that you do, making disciples and investing in relationships, will last into eternity. It may not make the front page of *USA Today*, but if you want to do something that will last forever, if you are ready to influence people in the best possible way, we think there is no better way to spend your life than making disciples of Jesus. Dive headfirst into the next chapters. Spend some time processing what you learn with others. And give yourself wholeheartedly to the movement Jesus launched and continues to lead today. Are you ready to join the Jesus revolution?

FOR REFLECTION AND CONVERSATION

1. What are your reflections on the concept of following Jesus' method of disciple making today? Is the thought new or old to you?

2. What is your reaction to Robert Coleman's belief that Jesus' disciple-making method was perfect? Explain.

3. What projects or causes will you have to give up in order to say "yes" to Jesus' invitation to participate in his disciple-making movement?

4. What are some ways in which churches deviate from Jesus' method of disciple making?

5. What can be done to help your church or ministry make disciples of Jesus?

Chapter 3

A DISCIPLE-MAKING EXAMPLE

> "For where two or three gather together as
> my followers, I am there among them."
> MATTHEW 18:20 (NLT)

> Love must be sincere. Hate what is evil; cling
> to what is good. Be devoted to one another in
> love. Honor one another above yourselves.
> ROMANS 12:9–10

Before we jump into the seven elements of a discipleship lifestyle, we want to start with a concrete, real-life example of what it means to make a disciple. We start here because, hands down, the most common question we are asked is, "What does this look like practically?" While there are many examples we could share, we've chosen to relate the story of how Josh goes about forming a men's discipleship group. This isn't just a group of guys who gather to study the Bible or talk about football. It's an intentional group that meets for a purpose, and it's structured around the seven elements that we just described.

We will unpack each of the elements in greater detail in the upcoming chapters. This chapter will give you a big-picture view. It's the "playbook" for starting a group, and even though the example is a men's group, the elements have been used for many different groups—women's groups, couples' (mixed gender) groups, young and old.

As with almost anything, you will need to think about your own context and then customize the transferable principles into your unique setting. You should also consider factors like your personality and your spiritual giftedness. Don't force yourself into a rigid model that doesn't fit your wiring. You may also want to talk with your church leaders to find out if your church has a specific model that they want you to follow.

> If you want a discipleship culture, you need lightweight, low-maintenance structure.
>
> **—ALEX ABSALOM**

That said, we know that this model works! The approach described here has been tested and found to be effective in our church and other churches we've shared it with. So we share it with confidence, knowing that the principles are biblical *and* practical.

There are five key steps to take when forming a disciple-making group. In this case, Josh was forming a men's group.

1. **Listen**
2. **Recruit**
3. **Prepare**
4. **Engage**
5. **Release**

STEP 1—LISTEN

The first step when forming a new discipleship group is to get in step with the Spirit ♦ and listen to God. This is the step that most people skip, but it is by far the most important aspect of forming a group. The groups that I led in the past that failed to multiply had one thing in common: *they were built in a prayerless, hurried fashion.* If you want the people in your group to grow, the Lord himself must lead the group. When you say "yes" to Jesus' call to become a disciple maker, you enter into a partnership with him where you work for him and with him.

When I joined the staff of Harpeth Christian Church a few years ago, my first priority was to develop relationships 👥 with a few men I could connect with on a deep-heart level. Three years prior to coming on staff at Harpeth, I had become an isolated pastor with no real friends. I knew a lot of people, but no one knew the real me. I felt tremendous pressure to project an image of strength and spiritual depth. I wanted people to see a confident, competent man of God when they looked at me. But living under unrealistic, self-imposed expectations was suffocating my soul. I was such a hypocrite in those days.

My prayer life was barely existent. Bible study was dull. I felt little to no burden to bless the poor or help unbelievers catch a glimpse of Jesus. A close look into my life during this season would've revealed a serious deficiency in spiritual fruit. The "check engine light" on my heart was blinking. This inner emptiness manifested itself most apparently in my inability (and stubborn unwillingness) to love my wife well. I was often harsh and inconsiderate with her. I confess that I was a compulsive idolater, and I routinely relied on created things to fill up the God-shaped hole in my soul. When I look in the rearview mirror of my life, I see a painful pattern. The enemy attacks us most viciously when we are alone, and an isolated heart is an unguarded heart. Satan is constantly firing arrows of fear, deception, and temptation toward us, and authentic Christ-centered community protects us from these attacks.

At the same time when I was feeling isolated and struggling with sinful patterns in my life, something else was happening. I was becoming increasingly disillusioned with the church, at least the church I had known and experienced. I was caught in a trap, giving my best emotional and creative energies to a church model that looked nothing like the ministry of Jesus. Programs trumped people. Tradition overwhelmed truth. The leadership had been hijacked by power-hungry men who cared more about preserving the institution than advancing the kingdom. Rather than trying to reach lost and hurting people, we competed with other churches in the area. When I looked at my ministry, I realized that I was spending an embarrassing amount of time babysitting believers who had little interest in knowing or being like Jesus. Eventually, something snapped. I could no longer feed the beast. It was as if God flipped a switch in my soul. There was no going back.

> Most of evangelism today is obsessed with getting someone to make a *decision*; the apostles, however, were obsessed with making *disciples*.
>
> —SCOT MCKNIGHT

I sensed God saying to me (no, not with an audible voice) that I didn't have to keep the ministry machine running, that a better and more transformative life was possible. The Lord graciously ushered me out of the shallow waters of cultural Christianity. I knew I needed to change. I could either maintain the status quo and invest in a way of life that wasn't producing fruit, or get on board with Jesus and the work he was doing of making disciples.

In the midst of this season of loneliness and disillusionment, the two story lines of my life converged, and God opened a door for me to serve at Harpeth Christian Church. The night before I walked into my new office at the church, I prayed this prayer:

Jesus, reveal five to seven men to me. Men with honest, hungry hearts. I need them every bit as much as they need me! Show me men with whom I can be totally open. I need friends who will know me as just another broken man who needs you, and not someone who seems to have it all together. When you make it clear who these men are, I commit to do everything I can to create an atmosphere of gospel vibrancy—where grace and truth flow freely, and you are the centerpiece of everything we do together. I've never done this before, so you'll have to do the leading! Give me eyes to see, Lord! Amen.

I prayed a version of this prayer every day, and around the ninety-day mark, God made it remarkably clear who these men were. I wrote their names down in a notebook and surrendered the list to Jesus. One by one, each man in his own way let me know (without my prompting) that he was searching for deep spiritual friendships.

Step one is simple, but you need to be patient and wait for the Lord. It begins with praying, asking God to do what God loves to do—call disciples with hungry hearts to follow him!

STEP 2—RECRUIT

My wife tells me that I tend to see the best in people, sometimes to a fault. I say that it can be a fault because I have a track record of overestimating good intentions and staying optimistic, even when things aren't looking good. In this case, I listened to my wife and took extra time to confirm that the names the Lord had given me were the people he wanted in our group.

I was very intentional, taking each man out for a meal or coffee to seek the Lord's will further. After small talk, I would share a bit of my story with them and ask a few basic, heart-probing questions, like, "What drives you as a man?" and "How do you define success in life?" and "What do you want people to say about you after you're gone?" and "If you could push a button that would instantly remove one struggle or challenge in your life, what would it be?" I didn't know the men very well at that point, and

I was a little afraid to ask such intense questions, but it paid off. Each man was genuinely encouraged that I cared enough to ask them questions like this and show concern for their lives.

> I found out the hard way that if we don't disciple people, the culture sure will.
>
> —ALAN HIRSCH

After I'd met with the men and had these conversations, I asked Bobby and the elders of the church and others to give me their appraisal of each man's character. Healthy disciple making involves many relationships, and I recommend getting input from people you trust who know those you are thinking of discipling. The leaders at our church want to develop disciple-making leaders, and we "go after" people who fit the AFTeR acronym:[1]

Available—Are they willing to make time for spiritual growth? Or are they distracted by other agendas?

Faithful—Do they have a track record of following through on commitments, or do they flake out?

Teachable—Are they open to learning new things, or are they closed-minded? Do they display a desire to grow in Christ, or are they content to remain where they are?

Reliable—Do they show up when they say they will? Are they honest?

More recently, we've referred to these four virtues by a fancy name: the discipleship quadrilateral. Whatever you choose to use, the bottom line is that people who don't fit this description aren't ready for authentic discipleship, so my advice: don't waste your time (or theirs). I know that may sound harsh. But you can save yourself from dead, lifeless groups where you are pulling teeth to get people to participate by seeking out those who are spiritually hungry. Jesus himself targeted those who were open to God—"Whoever has ears, let them hear" (Matt. 11:15).

Why are we spending so much time on matters of prayer and recruitment? Why such a slow and patient process of choosing? Most of the mistakes we've made as disciple makers are rooted in a lack of discernment. We overestimate people and their interest or abilities. Jesus didn't immediately invest in the Twelve. He spent an extended period of time with a larger group of people that included the Twelve. He took his time. Then prayed all night before he selected them (Luke 6:12–13). Then he spent three years with them and made sure they were ready before he commanded them to go and make disciples.

He didn't wait until they had it all together, but he didn't rush the process either. People should prove their character before we entrust them with the greatest cause on earth.

STEP 3—PREPARE

After listening and then asking the men to join the discipleship group, I invited all six men to meet me at a quiet, distraction-free place where we could share a meal and talk. As soon as everyone arrived, someone prayed for the meal, and I gave a short talk about our need for relationships that are close, life-giving, and distinctively Christ-centered. I admitted that even though I was a pastor, I really needed these relationships, 🖐 and I told them that I had prayed and felt led to pledge myself to each of them as a friend and brother in the Lord. Then I opened the floor and asked if they had anything to share.

What I heard that day confirmed that the Spirit 🔥 had engineered these connections and had called us to walk together. All of the men expressed similar desires and heart wounds. We were a motley crew: a pastor, an accountant, a corporate chef, a videographer, a web security expert, a financial planner, and a music professor. But we were all united by a common desire: to pursue Jesus together. After everyone shared,

I presented a group covenant that outlined some goals and guardrails for our group. This felt risky because it was more formal, and it may feel awkward for you as well. But relationships can feel awkward at times. Over the years, I've learned to err on the side of intentionality 🌼 and work through those awkward moments.

Remember, the Great Commission was catalyzed by the most brilliant man who ever lived. He had a plan. He worked the plan. He commanded his disciples to continue with the plan. And the plan worked! People don't float into spiritual maturity. Your group won't become close after one or two meetings. Spiritual growth and relational depth is a journey, 🏔 and you arrive at your destination if you are intentional and have a purpose. While God can work spontaneously and unexpectedly, the fruits of the Spirit 🔥 emerge from the soil of discipline and desire.

In case you are wondering, here is the covenant I presented at our lunch meeting that day:

+ + +

The purpose of this covenant is to express our shared convictions as a discipleship group. It should serve as a guardrail that provides trajectory and focus. It reminds us of the commitments we have made to Jesus and each other. It describes how we plan to live out our faith in the context of an intentionally Jesus-centered community.

By participating in this group, I agree with the following statements:

Jesus

1. I want to grow as a disciple of Jesus and learn how to honor and emulate him as a husband, father, son, brother, friend, and disciple maker.

Relationships

2. I understand that I will take direct, unfiltered feedback. I will do everything in my power to receive it in love and be transformed by it. I will avoid defensiveness, realizing that when I defend myself, I forfeit the opportunity to grow. I am committing to being open to examine myself—my personality, my past, my habits, the way I treat people. By God's grace and with the help of my brothers, I long to be more like Jesus.

Intentionality

3. I understand that I am committing to attending every meeting, arriving on time, and completing the assignments. No exceptions unless *providentially* hindered. We will present a schedule at our first official meeting, and I will manage my other commitments around the dates that are scheduled.

Journey

4. I understand that the mission of this group is to help each other become more like Jesus. This discipleship process is based upon Jesus, his teachings, and his method of making disciples.

Multiply

5. I further commit myself to, at some time in the future when Jesus lets me know that I am ready, becoming a disciple maker and forming a group like this myself.

Bible

6. I commit to get to know God better through his Word in this process. I will complete my reading assignments and prayerfully ask God to reveal himself to me.

Intentionality

7. (If married) I have discussed these things with my wife, and she fully supports my involvement. She willingly relinquishes the time that I will need to attend meetings and to do the readings and heart-work, with the goal of becoming a more Christlike husband and father.

Relationships

8. I recognize that in order to grow as followers of Jesus, I must openly share my life with this group—the good, the bad, and the ugly. I will disclose secrets, confess sins, and ask the group to help me overcome the areas of my life that have yet to be surrendered to the lordship of Jesus. I commit to total confidentiality. What is said in the group stays in the group. No exceptions.

 Spirit

9. I will pray for every member of this group daily. This discipline will enhance my connection to my brothers and will release the power of God in their lives.

 Relationships

10. I will not give unsolicited advice or try to solve someone else's problems during group meetings. I will listen attentively while others share and will respond when and if the person sharing requests feedback from me.

+ + +

Notice that I've already put the seven elements into use, right here from the beginning. I also gave anyone who didn't feel comfortable or couldn't commit an easy out. I told the men in several ways that it was totally fine if they didn't want to join a group like this. I encouraged them to pray about it and share our conversation with their wives (if they were married) and ask them to look over the covenant. We prayed and went our separate ways. One week later, I called each of them to gauge their interest.

Every single man was eager to get started.

I invited them to join me later that week to officially launch the group, and reminded them to bring back the covenant signed by each of them *and their wives*. They arrived early with their covenants in hand. It was one of the most spiritually exhilarating moments of my life, the result of months of prayer and intentionality. Jesus had heard my prayers and had responded in a clear and decisive way. My confidence in him skyrocketed.

STEP 4—ENGAGE

Now that you've taken steps to recruit and prepare the group, it's time to engage. Like any community, a healthy group establishes rhythms that foster unity and togetherness. Aside from penning the group covenant, we made all other decisions by exercising the discipline of group discernment. A spiritual mentor once told me, "God told *us* is more powerful than God told *me*." So rather than lead with a top-down, instructor-student posture, I try to come along-side the group to set a tone of transparency and gently guide the group when we get off track. The purpose of the covenant was to protect us from distractions, so we returned to it often.

But what does a typical week look like? Here's a rundown of how we do life together. 🏠

Relationships:

We met each Wednesday morning from 6:30 a.m. to 8:00 a.m. The first six meetings were devoted to giving each man an opportunity to share his unfiltered spiritual autobiography. ⛰

Journey:

I distributed a guide I put together each week to help the men get started. Here is the first week:

+ + +

Go to a quiet place and read Psalm 139.

We look back to see evidence of God at work to build our trust in him working in our future. Israelites looked back—they gathered stones, built altars, ate covenant meals, wrote and sang songs to remember the good works. God stories were told and repeated over and over again.

As you look back on your life's story, look for hints of God's movement, watching for his fingerprints. He uses seasons of pain and brokenness as well as peace and joy.

Look through the rearview mirror at your life. What would be some *defining moments* where you can see the grace of God at work? What moments caused a profound change in the direction of your life?

Now take those defining moments and narrow them down to five or so. Take each of these defining moments and write a paragraph or two elaborating on that defining moment. You have now written your story, telling how God has worked in your life to become who you are today for the sake of his purpose in you.

An example of God at work is the story of Joseph. Watching his father reconcile with his brother in Genesis 33 had to have been one of Joseph's defining moments as he became a reconciler with his own brothers for the sake of the nation of Israel.

+ + +

Once we'd worked through each man's life story, our group conversations followed a simple format:

1. We processed the previous week's reading assignment (about 45 minutes). 📖 *Bible*

2. We'd go around the room and do a heart-check, including an opportunity to confess sin and receive prayer (about 30 minutes). 🏠 *Relationships*

3. We'd spend additional time praying for each other (about 20 minutes). 🔥 *Spirit*

In addition to our weekly meetings, we leveraged technology to encourage each other by sending daily text messages and prayer requests. Every time someone would text a request for help, others would respond with words of affirmation, and other requests would *always* follow.

I'd also try to meet with each man, just the two of us, every four to six weeks to spend additional time together and strengthen our bond in Jesus. As of this writing, our group has been journeying together for over two years now, and I cannot imagine what my life would look like without these men. They know all about me, and they love me anyway. There is no pretense or posturing in this group. The atmosphere is grace saturated and unforced, safe and secure, transparent and transformative.

As I was finishing writing this chapter, a member of the group sent the following email to me:

> If we are to be disciples of Jesus who are being reformed and restored to become more like him, we need to have people in our lives, up close and personal.
>
> —JEFF VANDERSTELT

When our Wednesday morning group formed, I had no close friends. I had people that I cared for, and who cared for me, but I had never had a true open, reciprocal, Jesus-centered relationship with another man. I had never felt accepted for who I was, the good with the bad. I had never showed my vulnerabilities, my ugly side, to anyone outside my marriage. I was isolated, hidden, ashamed, scared, and lonely.

What our group has done for me can't be overestimated. I now have several close friends (brothers, really) who truly know me, and who love and accept me anyway. I can be myself, reveal my secrets, express my fears, and talk about real life in a safe environment. It is invigorating and freeing to be able to go beyond the facade of perfection and surface-level conversation with these men, and it has changed my life forever.

I have seen my desires and motivations change completely as a result of these friendships and the things we talk about and learn together. I never used to want to pray, to study the Bible expecting to meet God there, to read the great authors of the faith, or help others. Not really. Not in my innermost heart. But now I truly want those things. I am a more authentic friend, a more intentional father, a more caring teacher, and a more sensitive and diligent husband, and Jesus has used my men's group as a catalyst for these changes.

The group provides a forum to talk about how we might be better men in all facets. We look to Jesus for the example, and we learn from one another's triumphs and blunders. The group provides strong support, both emotionally and practically. We lean on each other when things are tough, and we celebrate together when things are great. And the group has shown me how to make friendships work outside the group as well. I now know how to pursue people, build deep and meaningful relationships, and relate to both believers and nonbelievers.

The group is now an indispensable part of my life, and I am so grateful that God has given me this life-giving thing that now touches all parts of my life.

It has been so encouraging to see the power of Jesus' method playing out in real-life relationships! But as wonderful as this is, it doesn't stop there. Life change is great, but disciple making is even better.

STEP 5—RELEASE

Disciple making is about reproduction and multiplication. It's about sending people out to disciple others, ⮂ and it feels risky and scary. Why? Because when something works well, we are reluctant to mess with it. Sending people out also exposes our idolatrous need for control. We may have doubts about those we've discipled, if they can really do it themselves. They may have a different personality or different gifts, and they won't lead their group *exactly* the way I do it.

There is no such thing as a one-size-fits-all approach to making disciples. That's why we talk about principles and elements rather than techniques. We must empower the people we're investing in to make disciples in a way that's consistent with their unique personality and spiritual giftedness. And remember—we aren't making disciples of ourselves. We're making disciples of Jesus. A studious, reflective introvert will engage people in discipleship differently than an outgoing, exuberant extrovert will. The introvert will draw people that share her affinity for deep thinking. The extrovert will use his gift of gab to disarm people and make them feel comfortable. The key here is freeing people to be themselves as they disciple others.

This last phase—multiplying ⮂ —should not be forced or contrived. The Holy Spirit ◊ will prompt a burden within a person or occasionally within an entire group and indicate that a time for reproduction is coming soon.

He will also guide the timing of when a person should invite people within their sphere of influence into discipling relationships. If we release people too soon, they may feel ill-prepared and quickly give up. On the other hand, if we hold on to them too long, we hinder them from taking risks and learning as they step out in faith to do what Jesus has ultimately created them to do. We speak from personal experience here. Let the Spirit lead.

Recently I spoke with a man who is reluctant to step into his calling as a disciple maker because, in his own words, he feels "spiritually inadequate." He grew up in a religious context that pressured him to perform . . . to get everything right. Now he struggles to take risks because he's terrified of failing. This pervasive fear of not measuring up has proven to be hazardous to his spiritual health.

What would I say to him? That it's one thing to believe in Jesus, but have you ever considered that Jesus *believes in us*? Jesus says to his disciples, "Let me tell you why you are here. You're here to be salt-seasoning that brings out the God-flavors of this earth. If you lose your saltiness, how will people taste godliness? . . . Here's another way to put it: You're here to be light, bringing out the God-colors in the world. God is not a secret to be kept. We're going public with this, as public as a city on a hill. If I make you light-bearers, you don't think I'm going to hide you under a bucket, do you? I'm putting you on a light stand. Now that I've put you there on a hilltop, on a light stand—shine! Keep open house; be generous with your lives. By opening up to others, you'll prompt people to open up with God, this generous Father in heaven" (Matt. 5:13–16, *The Message*).

When we send people out, it's natural to have fears and even some doubts. But we keep returning to one thing—it's not about us! When we act out of gratitude and obedience to Jesus, we can have confidence that Jesus will meet us with whatever faith we have if we trust him. Even if we have faith as small as a mustard seed, if Jesus is the object of our faith, we know he won't abandon us. That doesn't mean that everything always works out the way we think it should. But it does mean that even in failure and pain, God is present and he is at work.

Discipleship is a process of growth. For those of you who are parents with older children, you may recall what it was like when your children left home. At some point, you knew that for your son or daughter to take the next step toward maturity, they would need to strike out on their own. That doesn't mean that your relationship ends—it just changes. There are times when someone you've discipled will need you for advice or will call you up for coffee to talk. It won't always go perfectly. But the alternative is a prolonged adolescence, the equivalent of the thirty-year-old who doesn't leave home and allows Mom and Dad to take care of him all day. Sadly, when it comes to disciple making, our churches are filled with immature disciples who have never learned how to own their faith.

In this chapter, we've provided a specific example of how to enter into the process of disciple making, but the point is not the specifics of the model—it's the steps of the process. We simply find it helpful to flesh it out with real-world examples, rather than talking in generalities. In the next section, we'll take a closer look at the seven elements of a discipleship lifestyle. But before we go there, we have one last thing we want to share with you.

We've found it incredibly helpful to step back from our assumptions about discipleship, those mental pictures we create that limit where and when disciple making can occur. The truth is that Jesus discipled people everywhere he went, and he did it differently in different contexts. The following diagram should give

you a sense of the different types of discipling relationships Jesus had with people. We looked through the Gospels and combined what we saw there with insights from academic studies that have identified various social contexts in which we live—public, social, personal, transparent, divine—to better understand how Jesus made disciples in each context:

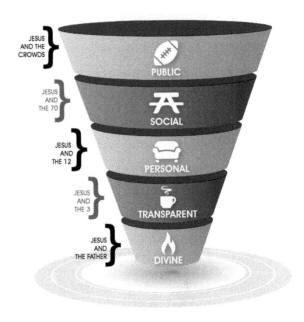

discipleship.org

From the book *Discipleship That Fits*
by Harrington and Absalom

- *PUBLIC Context: A common example of this in our church context today is the Sunday gathering* that typically has a hundred-plus people. Some of the disciple-making elements—like using the Bible and prayer and worship in reliance on the Holy Spirit—can be strong here. But this context is not conducive to the deeper life change and personal attention that people need to grow.

- *SOCIAL Context: Many churches today have developed something called a missional community* that is a smaller gathering of 20 to 70 people who meet for a common purpose and to develop interpersonal relationships. This is a perfect-size gathering for getting to know people and sharing snapshots of life to build a common affinity. A missional community is an extended family of relationships centered around Jesus that goes and makes disciples among a specific group of people.

- *PERSONAL Context: This is one of the most common contexts today for disciple making and has been very popular over the past three decades. Small groups* are usually groups of eight to fifteen people, and they provide disciple making in the personal context. People get to know one another personally, sharing struggles at times, but usually not intimately. As wonderful as the small group setting is for exercising spiritual gifts and going deeper in relationships, it is still sometimes too

large for getting into patterns of sin and addressing heart issues.

- *TRANSPARENT Context: This is the most transformative context for disciple making. There are many different names for the relational connections at this level, including discipleship groups, accountability groups, and one-on-one* gatherings. This can range from two people meeting to a smaller group of up to six people. Any more than this number and transparency becomes more difficult. The "triad" of three people is a popular group for this context, offering the intimacy of a one-on-one group with the shared accountability that comes when you have more than two people. Jesus had a group of three men—Peter, John, and James—and he shared things with this group that he did not share with the others.

- *DIVINE Context: This is simply your personal walk alone* with God. Sometimes this isn't included in discussions of discipleship or disciple making, but we believe this is a mistake. This context covers aspects of spiritual formation that include spiritual disciplines we engage as individuals, like personal prayer, Bible reading, meditation, fasting, and others. Many leaders, including names like

Dallas Willard and John Ortberg, focus on discipleship at this context.

As you can see, there is no "one size" that fits everyone in disciple making. We have given you just one model for disciple making in the *transparent* space in this chapter. But there are many more models for this space. And there are multiple models for the other spaces.

Some discipling spaces are better suited for someone who is not yet a Christian; others are ideal for mature disciples who want to grow and learn. Some groups will emphasize Bible study, some will emphasize prayer, some will emphasize relationships and confession, and some will emphasize mission. You may need to explore through trial and error and with the help of the leaders in your church to find the kind of group that is best suited for you as a disciple maker in your context.

We say this so you don't give up if you try and it doesn't seem to work the first time. You may find that you are better meeting one-on-one than leading a small group of ten to twelve. Or you disciple best by creating an adult education class/group or preaching to the gathered church.

In whatever size group you find yourself serving—from a one-on-one relationship to a Sunday gathering—you will find that one or more of the seven elements will be key in that context. All of these elements are foundational to Jesus' method and useful for disciple making today, in whatever context we operate.

PART 2

THE SEVEN ELEMENTS OF A DISCIPLESHIP LIFESTYLE

Chapter 4

RELATIONSHIPS

> "Your love for one another will prove to
> the world that you are my disciples."
> JOHN 13:35 (NLT)

It's not a stretch to say that the whole Bible is about relationships. The Bible speaks not just of our relationship with God, but about our relationships with other people as well. Consider the Ten Commandments. On the surface, they look like a list of rules, but a better way of thinking of them is as the guardians of relationships. By observing the first four commandments, we honor and protect our relationship with God.

1. You shall have no other gods before me.

2. You shall not make idols.

3. You shall not take the name of the LORD your God in vain.

4. Remember the Sabbath day by keeping it holy.

And commandments five through ten address our relationships with others.

5. Honor your father and your mother.

6. You shall not murder.

7. You shall not commit adultery.

8. You shall not steal.

9. You shall not bear false witness against your neighbor.
10. You shall not covet.

Or consider that when someone asked Jesus to tell him the greatest commandment in the law, Jesus spoke about loving relationships with God and with others.

> "'Love the Lord your God with all your heart and with all your soul and with all your mind.' This is the first and greatest commandment. And the second is like it: 'Love your neighbor as yourself.' All the Law and the Prophets hang on these two commandments" (Matt. 22:37–40).

According to Jesus, you can summarize most of the Bible as God's plan for us to have healthy, loving relationships with him and with others. In the first story of the first book of the Bible, God makes sure that we catch this. We hear him say with his own voice that we were created to connect with other people:

> "It is not good for the man to be alone" (Gen. 2:18 NLT).

This means that our desire and capacity for relationships are part of our hard wiring.

Consider your own life right now. Are you sharing your life with other disciples? How are you spiritually connected to the body of Christ? Are you in need of someone to disciple you? Or, if you have been discipled by someone already, do you have anyone in your life that you are *currently* discipling? If not, I wouldn't be surprised to hear that you are feeling dry or unproductive in your faith and in need of a spiritual tune-up.

> Discipleship is all about living life together rather than just one structured meeting per week.
>
> —FRANCIS CHAN

Scripture gives us many examples of people investing in relationships with other people. We all know that it's one thing to sit in a church gathering—watching and listening—but it's another thing to be taught about Jesus with a few others who know you well. In the context of personal relationships, questions can be asked, real-life stories can be shared, sin can be confessed, accountability can be offered, and encouragement can be given. There is a greater capacity for truth transfer. Coincidentally, this describes how Jesus made his own disciples. Jesus' ministry teaches us that disciple making is a relational process, one built on trust.

Dr. Coleman, in his book *The Master Plan of Evangelism,* assumes that the *incarnation* of Jesus was the starting point and foundation of Jesus' method, but he did not explicitly start with it and state it is his book. By this principle he means that Jesus entered fully into human life, especially in relationships with others. And this trajectory of the incarnation, taking on everything "human" to fully identify with and relate to us, was characteristic of Jesus' ministry and his methods. Coleman states that if he were outlining his principles today—over fifty years after writing what became one of the most influential Christian books of the last hundred years—this is the only principle he would add to the book and emphasize. He said that he made the mistake of just assuming it.[1]

Jesus' method started when he entered into the world of others and built relationships with people. He didn't just come to be a human being; he came to be a human being in relationship with people and show us what it really means to live a godly life, fully alive to God and people. And because we are blind and unaware of how to do this, he first came into our lives to show us how much God loves us.

Coleman had it right, and we tell everyone who wants to follow Jesus' method today to begin the same way. Start by entering into the lives of others. Form relationships with the heart of Jesus. Show them how much God loves them. Coleman puts it this way:

Nothing disarms a person like love. Everyone likes to be loved and for someone to express love to them in tangible ways. When you know you're loved, you'll listen and open up. It was Christ loving people, His service to them, His ministry to them—healing the sick, opening the eyes of the blind, delivering those possessed by demons, teaching them about the Kingdom of God—that drew people to Him, and the same is true with our ministries. You have an audience with everybody who knows they're loved and knows you care about them. The incarnation is the foundation upon which we must begin to express our life in Christ. It's a beginning place to fulfill the Great Commission, starting with reaching out just as Jesus did in making disciples.[2]

Motives matter. If you're doing all this to fulfill an inner need to accomplish something or to prove to others that you are a good leader or really smart, it won't last. We don't engage others in relationship because it proves that we are effective disciple makers. True discipleship begins as a response to God's love. God's love humbles and transforms us into people who are freed up from focusing on ourselves to truly love others. And as we love others, we experience the joy of God. All of this produces the fruit of God-honoring relationships. Relationships lie at the heart of God's nature as a Trinity, and they are at the heart of our created purpose as human beings. Jesus came to restore relationship, so it's no surprise that relationships are one of the most important things talked about in the Bible.[3]

> The ways Jesus goes about loving and saving the world are personal: nothing disembodied, nothing abstract, nothing impersonal. Incarnate, flesh and blood, relational, particular and local. The ways employed in our North American culture are conspicuously impersonal: programs, organizations, techniques, and general guidelines, informational, detached from place. In matters of ways and means, the vocabulary of numbers is preferred over names, ideologies crowd out ideas, the gray fog of abstraction absorbs the sharp particularities of the recognizable face and the familiar street.
>
> —EUGENE PETERSON[4]

MAKE LOVE THE ULTIMATE THING

When we say that Jesus put a priority on relationships, we don't just mean that Jesus was always hanging out with people (which he was). Jesus invested time with people. He ate with them. Talked with them. He got to know the people he was discipling. He entered into their world, and he invited them into his world. Notice the tenderness in his interactions with Mary, Martha, and Lazarus. We get only snapshots, but these pictures reflect a level of depth and intimacy that is possible only after knowing someone for months and years (John 11). That's what we want to experience with those we seek to disciple.

But there is even more. Throughout his life, Jesus teaches that a *certain kind of relationship* is needed, one that is grounded in self-giving love (the Greek word *agape* is used to refer to this love in the Bible; we simply call it "Jesus-like" love). We see this love in the life of Jesus as he sacrifices himself, constantly putting the needs of others first. This is not just his death on the cross, but the culmination and natural conclusion of how he lived every day. Every day of Jesus' life was a reflection of the cross, expressing the Father's will in obedience and loving lost sinners by laying down his own needs and wants to meet those of others. Jesus gives us this vitally important summary of how his disciples should reflect him in John 13:34–35:

"A new command I give you: Love one another. As I have loved you, so you must love one another. By this everyone will know that you are my disciples, if you love one another."

Notice what Jesus says: "as I have loved you." Jesus-like love is something that we first experience in the context of being discipled by God through the Holy Spirit and God's Word and in the context of community through a discipleship relationship with others in the body of Christ. But love is not just the environment that makes discipleship happen, it is also the *evidence* of true discipleship. And so living a life that reflects this kind of love becomes our highest priority as disciple makers and disciples.

PAUSE AND PONDER

Why is self-giving, agape love so important to Jesus? How do we make it the ultimate focus, as the Bible teaches?

The Bible tells us that this is how we know what love is: Jesus Christ laid down his life for us. Notice what follows immediately—the first implication of truly understanding what Jesus has done for us. *We ought to lay down our lives for our brothers and sisters* (1 John 3:16). If we truly understand what love is, we cannot keep it to ourselves. It transforms us into people who willingly sacrifice ourselves for the sake of others. It's important that we get this right because there are many other good things in the Bible that might appear to be just as important. But love is not just one among many good things—it's central.

Some time ago, a friend posted something on Facebook. It was posted as a response to a political flashpoint on sex and gender that had just hit the news, but we think it captures much of the heart of Jesus in helping us to set our priorities.

Confused about the "Christian response" to social issues? Here's a handy reference list.

Male—love them.	Addict—love them.
Female—love them.	Sober—love them.
Unsure—love them.	Believer—love them.
Gay—love them.	Unbeliever—love them.
Straight—love them.	Unsure—love them.
Unsure—love them.	

In 1 Corinthians 13, God shows us several alternatives to ministry without Jesus-like love. There are people who talk a great deal about the Holy Spirit. Others claim experiences of the Holy Spirit are what matters most. But writing under inspiration, the apostle Paul tells us that "if I speak in the tongues of men or of angels, *but do not have love,* I am only a resounding gong or a clanging cymbal" (1 Cor. 13:1, emphasis added).

> To be fully known and fully loved is the most healing gift one human being can give another.
>
> —JOHN ORTBERG

Paul seems to anticipate objections here. After all, some might reply, "Truth, orthodoxy, correct belief, loyalty to the doctrines of Scripture, and the Reformation confessions are most important." And we'd agree that biblical doctrine is vital and must necessarily inform how we love people. Love and truth are two sides of the same coin, and we must fight the good fight of the faith to defend the truth. But don't miss the point of this passage. Paul goes on to say, "If I have the gift of prophecy and can fathom all mysteries and all knowledge, . . . but do not have love, I am nothing" (1 Cor. 13:2).

Some might argue that having faith is the key. But Paul anticipates that as well: "If I have a faith that can move mountains, but do not have love, I am nothing" (1 Cor. 13:2). No matter how gifted we may be in understanding truth or exercising faith, Jesus-like love is the single most important reflection of Christlikeness and discipleship within the church.

Others focus on the importance of service. Wait, isn't serving others how we love them? Those with the gift of mercy or those drawn to social justice and serving the poor will say, "The authentic mark of a true believer is what we do, especially in service to the poor and the needy." But service does not always spring from godly love for others! It can be done for a variety of motives. Love is what matters: "If I give all I possess to the poor and give over my body to hardship that I may boast, but do not have love, I gain nothing" (1 Cor. 13:3).

The most important sign of authentic discipleship is Jesus-like love.

- It is not a worship experience.
- It is not experiences of the Holy Spirit.
- It is not correct doctrine.
- It is not faith.
- It is not service to the poor and needy.

All of these are good things. And we can do all of them over the course of a lifetime and still miss what it means to be a disciple of Jesus. Jesus-like love is both the environment and the fruit that God wants to see produced in his church. It tops the list of the fruits that the Holy Spirit grows in our lives (Gal. 5:22).

The apostle Paul describes Jesus-like love for us this way:

> Love is patient, love is kind. It does not envy, it does not boast, it is not proud. It does not dishonor others, it is not self-seeking, it is not easily angered, and it keeps no record of wrongs. Love does not delight in evil but rejoices with the truth. It always protects, always trusts, always hopes, always perseveres. Love never fails (1 Cor. 13:4–8).

As we trust and follow Jesus and seek to help others to trust and follow Jesus, we must never forget that the true sign of authentic godliness in our midst will be the Jesus-like love we show to one another. We want our lives and our churches to radiate the great love that God has so freely shown to us.

Not too long ago, a couple left our church a year or two after they had joined. They started attending as singles and were part of one of our discipleship communities. They were loved and served exceptionally well by our church. Our leaders gave them extra time and support in dealing with personal challenges and issues with their extended family. This couple decided to get married, and their discipleship leader and the entire group helped them prepare for the ceremony. They were freely given premarriage counseling, decorations for the event, food, music, a minister to lead the service—everything you might need to have a great wedding event. The wedding cost them almost nothing. It was an especially wonderful ceremony, an expression of Jesus-like love.

A month or two later, they left the church.

When one of our leaders met with them to ask why they were leaving, they said that our Sunday gatherings were not Spirit-led enough for them. I (Bobby) had a chance to meet with some of their extended family for lunch shortly afterward. They hinted at the same thing to me. I listened for a little while, but eventually I had to clarify something for them. "You say Spirit led," I said to them, "but really, what do you mean?" Their response described a hunger for a certain emotional experience from their past. "The most important sign of being Spirit led," I said, "is not a certain emotional engagement in the music in a church service; it's Jesus-like love!"

Then I asked them, "Where in the Bible do you find it saying that an emotional experience in a church service is a better sign of the Holy Spirit's presence than people laying down their lives and sacrificing themselves to care for people?"

To be clear, I'm not against experiential worship or advocating for a specific style of music here. That's not my point. But I find that very often, we focus on surface-level details like this in determining what it means to be authentic and biblical. Instead, let's look at what the Bible actually teaches! What matters to God? The Bible is clear that our Jesus-like love is to be the foundation and fruit of everything we do in making disciples. Because love as given to us by God is the ultimate sign of his presence and work, love is our priority as disciple makers. We pursue a life of love, a mind-set of love (Eph. 5:1–2). In this life most of us will not do great things by worldly standards. We may only do "small" things, but we can do them with lots of love. That's okay! It doesn't matter what we do, big or small, if God's love is the distinguishing trait of what we do.

Here are some questions to guide you if you want this Jesus-like love to lead your disciple making.

- Before reading this book, what would you have said is the most important expression of your faith? Why?
- Do you personally believe that it was ultimately love that motivated Jesus to make disciples?
- What would it take for Jesus-like love to be your ultimate expression of faith?
- What will it take for love to be your motivation in disciple making, and what will that look like?
- What might get you sidetracked from developing Jesus-like love?

MAKE IT LIFE ON LIFE

When I (Josh) moved to Franklin, Tennessee, seven years ago, I met with some older, seasoned church leaders and asked them to help me better understand the spiritual climate of the area I had just moved to. One of the questions I asked was, "What is the main barrier that keeps people from growing and maturing in Christ?" The answer was unanimous. They all said, "Isolation."

Despite having a thousand friends on Facebook or Instagram and being "connected" 24/7, the truth is that we live in a culture of shallow relationships. We'd rather watch actors pretend to engage in real relationships on TV than forge safe, vulnerable connections of our own. Some time ago, a piece in the *Los Angeles Times* written by Neal Gabler grabbed my attention.[5] The last paragraph of the piece took my breath away:

> The fact is that we miss the friendships we no longer have, and we know that Facebook or emails cannot possibly compensate for the loss. So we sit in front of our television sets and enjoy the dream of friendship instead: a dream where we need never be alone, where there are a group of people who would do anything for us, and where everyone seems to understand us to our very core, just like Jerry and George, Chandler and Joey, Carrie and her girls, or the members of the McKinley High glee club. It is a powerful dream, and it is one that may now be the primary pleasure of television.

Today, Americans have on average fewer friends than they had a decade ago. In the place of actual friends and confidants, we have faux friendships on social media, or we live vicariously through television.

But God wants so much more for us. We need to be intentional about this, to break through our culture of isolation and create the relationships Jesus demonstrated and for which people are longing. Below are four statements that capture why relationships are so essential—more than programs, curriculum, or the method you use—to the task of discipleship:[6]

1. Without a relationship, we are just passing on information. This is not discipleship.
2. We cannot do what Jesus wants us to do in the Great Commission without doing it the way Jesus tells us to do life-on-life relationships.
3. A church must create it—relational environments for discipleship, or people will seek other ways to grow in relationships outside the church.
4. You can impress people for a few minutes through an interesting lecture or a good sermon—but long-term life change happens through relationships.

We stress these four points because we were both told in seminary, by more than one professor, that it was unwise to get too close to the people at church. They warned us against developing close relationships with the people we served as pastors. They encouraged us to look outside the church for authentic connections. And we have personally known dozens of pastors and church leaders who have fallen prey to enslaving sins. Guess what they all had in common? They all walked alone. They were isolated, lacking deep relationships with other people. Our faith grows, deepens, and flourishes in community with other believers. It withers in isolation.

When we describe the need for "relationships" as the vehicle for biblical discipleship, we want to be clear that the local church is essential. We need to recover a New Testament understanding of church, where we stop seeing the church as a building or an institution and recognize that the essence of the church is our relational connectedness. The word *church* is a translation of the Greek word *ekklesia*, which literally means "those called out." In biblical times, it described "the called out people," "the assembly," "the gathering," or "the congregation."[7] It is never used in the Bible to refer to a building. In fact, church buildings did not even appear until hundreds of years after the Bible was written. The best way to think of church is to see it as a large support community or, even better, an extended family of the disciples of Jesus.

We read in Acts 2:42–47 the first description of a gathering of believers—a church:

They devoted themselves to the apostles' teaching and to fellowship, to the breaking of bread and to prayer. Everyone was filled with awe at the many wonders and signs performed by the apostles. All the believers were together and had everything in common. They sold property and possessions to give to anyone who had need. Every day they continued to meet together in the temple courts. They broke bread in their homes and ate together with glad and sincere hearts, praising God and enjoying the favor of all the people. And the Lord added to their number daily those who were being saved.

Though the times were different, this is still a very striking description, don't you think? The Bible says that these early Christians "devoted" themselves to teaching, fellowship, breaking bread, and praying together. That's a perfect description of what we mean by discipling relationships. This is not your typical "go to a worship gathering once a week and cross that off the list" thing. Church was a gathering of disciples for the purpose of discipleship, growing more deeply in God's Word, in community, and in spiritual and relational connectedness.

We need to recover this understanding of church again today. If we want to make disciples like the early church made disciples, we need to look more like the early church. Not by re-creating their cultural context, but by looking at how they related to one another and what they did together to grow together as disciples. We need to look at our own cultural context and find creative ways to share life with others, making much of Jesus and joining him in his cause to heal and restore the world. Discipleship is life on life, heart to heart.

> The early church made special effort to bring new converts, without delay, into close relationships with other believers.
>
> —ROBERT COLEMAN

Here are some questions to guide you as you consider your own life. As you think about these questions, pray that God would give you ideas and guidance to embrace this call to life-on-life disciple making:

- As you read the description of the church in Acts 2, what most inspires you?
- How isolated are you right now from others? Who in your life knows how you are doing right now, what you are celebrating, and what you are struggling with?
- When was the last time you shared your struggles and dreams with someone?

- Why is isolation such a big problem for people today? What are some of the challenges you face in growing in relationship with others?
- We all have different personalities. How might introverts and extroverts engage in this in different ways?
- What kind of lifestyle changes would you prayerfully consider making so that you can more fully enter into life-on-life discipling relationships?

GO DEEP

Several years ago, I (Bobby) led a gathering of several pastors at Real Life Ministries in Post Falls, Idaho. We were there to discuss this question of relationships and to look for ways to better emphasize relationships in our churches and ministries. In this meeting and in others since then, I've noticed that whenever we talk about an emphasis on relationships, some pastors get nervous. They think that emphasizing relationships means that we are going to diminish the deeper things of the faith. They associate a deeper faith with more knowledge of the doctrines of the Bible or theology. Please don't misunderstand what we're saying. I believe strongly in Bible study. I completed four degrees in the Bible myself, and I'm very committed to the Bible and understand our need to study and learn the Bible. But knowledge of the Bible alone will not lead to deep life transformation.

At that gathering, my friend Luke Yetter was teaching, and he began sharing story after story, giving examples of everyday people in his church engaging in life-on-life disciple making. He described people coming to Christ in baptisms, marriages saved, suicidal people being rescued—and on and on he went. He also described some heartbreaking times when things did not work out, when people left or relationships went sour.

But instead of portraying these challenges as failures, he pointed out that one of the realities of a discipling relationship is getting up close and dealing with serious people problems. He told about a man who had a lot of problems—spiritually, physically, and relationally—who attended his small group during the week. The problems were quite severe, and, like many of those gathered, I began to feel a sense of despair for this man. Suddenly, Luke stopped his story. "When we talk about going deep," he said, "that is what I mean. When it costs us a lot to really love people, how deep do we want to go? That kind of depth will reveal the depth of our faith as true disciples of Jesus."

Many of the core values that drive our culture, both inside and outside the church, severely limit our ability to go deep with others. We've internalized many of these values, sometimes without realizing that they aren't biblical. The truth is that real, authentic relationships require investments of time and energy. There are risks. As disciple makers, we need to return to the concept of spiritual friendship that was evident in the early church.

We will not survive as faithful disciples of Jesus through the trials of the faith without close spiritual friends, brothers and sisters who will graciously support us when we fail and struggle, friends who will celebrate together with us the joys of following Jesus. The need for these friendships is especially true for those who struggle with addictions, marriage problems, living as celibate singles, or overcoming habits of indwelling sin—and yet sincerely want to follow Jesus. It's going to take close relationships. We are going to have to remake our churches to be more like the early church if we are going to truly disciple people. Close, intimate, and enduring friendships—where we truly become brothers and sisters for each other—are essential.[8]

Do you have any friends? If you do, you understand that to make (and keep) a real friend, you need to invest time and effort into someone, and that person must be open to this and allow us in. You'll need to make time to cultivate this friendship, and you'll have to expend effort to get to know this person. You'll need to take some risks and share your heart as well, letting him or her get to know you as well. Friends see the good, the bad, and the ugly. But as time passes, trust grows. That's how genuine friendships are born.

Relationships like this are anything but convenient. They won't happen in a crowded schedule or a hurried life. If you find yourself saying, "I just don't have time to connect with that person," you probably should take a hard look at your priorities and commitments. Where are you currently focusing your time and energy? Are you more concerned about completing tasks and getting work done than with getting to know people? While we are each wired differently, we must not forget that our focus is on loving people—not checking off a task list. Jesus didn't view people as obstacles or distractions that hindered his ministry. People *were* his ministry.

We hope you catch the vision for relationships. We hope you see that this is where Jesus focused his time and his effort and that it is the best vehicle for life transformation and discipleship. And we know that for many of you reading this, it will require some changes and sacrifices to reprioritize your life to focus on new relationships. Here are some questions to guide you as you seek to do this:

- Where do you have time in your life right now to invest in other people? If you cannot see how this fits, take a look at the things you are doing where you might bring more of a relational focus. For example, if you are at your job all day, could you intentionally develop relationships with co-workers over a lunchtime Bible study? In addition, consider some things you are doing that you might need to stop doing to free up time for relationships.

- How comfortable are you when things "get real"? What are some ways you might begin to grow in your ability to become more comfortable with other people?

- How would you rate your ability to deal with conflicts without giving up on a person? What are some ways you can grow in this area? If you aren't sure, consider talking to a pastor or church leader to see if they have any materials to recommend to help you.

- How far are you willing to go to be a friend to someone who is different from you so you can give them the support they need to make it as a disciple of Jesus?

Nothing can be more cruel than that leniency which abandons others to their sin.

—DIETRICH BONHOEFFER

MAKE DISCIPLE MAKING RELATIONAL

To this point, we've largely been speaking about relationships with other Christian believers in a local church. Even if we are very different ethnically, socially, or in other ways, we share a common commitment to love Jesus and grow as his disciple. But what about those who aren't yet believers? Can we develop relationships with them that focus on discipleship? Yes! In fact, this is the best way to introduce someone to Jesus and set them on a biblical trajectory for discipleship from the very beginning.

If we believe that we might be able to reach someone who does not know Jesus, or if we believe that one of us might be the person to help someone grow as a disciple, we approach that relationship the same way as we do with a believer. Our friend Alex Absalom has helped us to see that disciple making—for non-Christians and Christians alike—begins at "hello." Even in the midst of writing this book, I (Bobby) spent time with our neighbors at a picnic my wife had organized. Nine of the ten neighborhood families showed up, several of them non-Christians.

Through gatherings like this, our family has begun several discipling relationships with neighbors. My wife meets early on Sundays with two of our neighbors, and my son is in a men's small group with another neighbor who is not yet a Christian. My wife has helped one of the women learn how to trust and follow Jesus through the heartache of a divorce. Another woman had previously divorced her husband, and then, through a relationship with my wife, they began a Bible study. After they met, this woman decided that she should not have divorced her husband in the first place, and God worked a special miracle. They are now in the process of marital reconciliation.

People who do not know Jesus are looking for authentic community just as much as those who already know Jesus, and relationships offer the ideal setting for sustained life change. Relationships are where we recover from the effects of sin and receive the support we need when we struggle. Community is where God does his best work. Nobody flourishes when they stand alone. Nobody breaks the power of sin or overcomes an addiction by going it alone. Nobody experiences a deeper life with God when they stand alone. And nobody can become a disciple by being alone. We learn how Jesus rescues us in relationships.

In emphasizing relationships and the need to develop spiritual friendships with other Christians and nonbelievers, we don't want to give the impression that this all just happens without organization. Disciple makers need organizational structures in the church, but—and this is key—those structures should *support* relational discipleship. Often this requires some shifts in structure or programming and might be easier to do in a new church plant, but traditional churches can also make adjustments without changing everything they are doing. Several helpful and important books have been written on this subject to guide church leaders in making those changes.[9]

The important thing is that the church structures should be adapted to support the work of intentional, relational discipleship, rather than just educational discipleship. The following chart shows more clearly some of the differences between the approach we are sharing (intentional relational discipleship) versus a more traditional approach that has been popular over the last several hundred years (educational discipleship).[10]

EDUCATIONAL DISCIPLESHIP	INTENTIONAL RELATIONAL DISCIPLESHIP
Requires attention to Scripture	A personal relationship pointed to Jesus
Scripture and Holy Spirit	Scripture, the Holy Spirit, and relationships
Head	Head, heart, and hands
Academic	Teaching / modeling / coaching
Emphasizes factual knowledge	Emphasizes life application
Information	Transformation
Content	Supportive relationship
No breaking of bread Start and stop time / quick	Breaking of bread Meet in homes daily / takes time
Teacher has all the answers	Let's figure it out together
Large group	Small group
Building / campus	Home
Lesson is the agenda	Doing life together
Setting is formal	Setting is casual

PAUSE AND PONDER

What kind of setting were you discipled in? Did you learn about Jesus in a class context or one that was more informal and relational?

We understand that in contrasting these two approaches, we are drawing out the extremes. But we think it is important to point out these contrasts because the educational model has been so dominant for so long. In our experience, it requires an intentional and dedicated effort to push toward a more relational discipleship approach. It requires some creativity as well, so you'll want to explore ideas for how to make this work in your own context. Discuss this with others in your church or community. Remember—we can't do it on our own. God does his best work as we live in community with others, working through our relationships and applying the truth of God's Word through the power of the Holy Spirit.

- Remember that cultivating relationships takes time. There will be interactions and shared experiences that will feel unproductive, but be patient. Don't underestimate the power of just being present and available to someone.

- Healthy relationships aren't forced, and there is no agenda other than to love well and point each other to Jesus. The people we're discipling aren't projects to manage or problems to solve.

- Jesus spent the bulk of his time investing in a few people. He did this for a reason. He took this little group and changed the world. Now it's our turn!

- Paul summed it up for the Ephesians (5:1–2 ESV): "Therefore be imitators of God, as beloved children. And walk in love, as Christ loved us and gave himself up for us, a fragrant offering and sacrifice to God." We will say it again: Discipleship, first and foremost, is relational; it is making time to relationally engage people and love them as Jesus loved.

> Jesus said you are to love one another as I have loved you, a love that will possibly lead to the bloody, anguish gift of yourself, a love that forgives seven times seven, that keeps no record of wrong. This is the criterion, sole norm, the standard of discipleship.
>
> —BRENNAN MANNING

FOR REFLECTION AND CONVERSATION

1. Why is a commitment to relationships so important in disciple making? Are you willing to make the relationship with the person(s) you are discipling a priority?

2. What does it mean to share your whole life (the good, the bad, and the ugly) with other people? How have you encountered Jesus through other people sharing their whole life?

3. How do you plan to disciple others in the context of biblical relationship?

4. What other time commitments are you willing to give up so that you can invest in discipling relationships?

5. Why is a church community important in discipling relationships? How will you integrate church community in your discipleship plan and make it a priority?

Chapter 5

JESUS

> He is the one we proclaim, admonishing and
> teaching everyone with all wisdom, so that we
> may present everyone fully mature in Christ.
>
> COLOSSIANS 1:28

U2's Bono made a striking statement during an interview: "I think a defining question for a Christian is: Who was Christ?" He went on to say,

And I don't think you're let off easily by saying a great thinker or a great philosopher, because actually he went around saying he was the Messiah. That's why he was crucified. He was crucified because he said he was the Son of God. So, he either, in my view, was the Son of God, or he was . . . nuts. . . . And, I find it hard to accept that whole millions and millions of lives, half the earth, for two thousand years have been touched, have felt their lives touched and inspired by some nutter.[1]

If you want to make disciples, nothing is more important than who you believe Jesus is and what you teach about him. What we believe about Jesus determines what it means to be his disciple. Bill Hull often explains it this way:

"The Jesus we preach and the gospel we uphold determine the disciple we get."[2] Stop and read that last statement again. What do you believe and teach about Jesus? That will decide the kind of disciple you are becoming and forming.

We agree with Bono that Jesus was not "some nutter." But that leads to several questions that beg to be asked today. What does it really mean to say, "Jesus is the Son of God" or "Jesus is the Messiah"? Popular Christian writer Kevin DeYoung wrote a widely read blog post where he listed fifteen different ways Jesus is presented today. Here are five we commonly hear about.[3]

- There's *Republican Jesus* who is against tax increases and activist judges and for family values and owning firearms.
- There's *Democrat Jesus* who is against Wall Street and Walmart and for reducing our carbon footprint and spending other people's money.
- There's *Therapist Jesus* who helps us cope with life's problems, heals our past, tells us how special we are and not to be too hard on ourselves.
- There's *Starbucks Jesus* who sits all day in coffee shops, loves spiritual conversations, drives a hybrid, and goes to film festivals.
- There's *Open-Minded Jesus* who accepts every viewpoint from every person,

regardless of how absurd it might be. He doesn't, however, accept people who are not as open-minded as he is.

Seriously, if we are helping people trust and follow Jesus, which Jesus are we introducing them to? Have we created Jesus in our own image, to suit our sensibilities, or do we know the real Jesus as he is revealed in the Bible? Again, if we want people to follow Jesus, be changed by Jesus, and be committed to his mission, we need clarity on Jesus' identity.

> It's impossible to be a disciple or follower of someone and not end up like that person. Jesus said, "A disciple is not above his teacher, but everyone when he is fully trained will be like his teacher" (Luke 6:40). That's the whole point of being a disciple of Jesus: we imitate Him, carry on His ministry, and become like Him in the process.
>
> —FRANCIS CHAN

We start with the Bible, but our reading and study should be coupled with insights from history, the creeds, and an understanding of what the greater church has taught and believed for the last two millennia. We encourage you to do some study on your own, but for now we suggest that you consider these six statements about Jesus as you seek to be a disciple who makes disciples of Jesus. These are not exhaustive. It would be impossible to fully explain the glorious realities of Jesus in one book, let alone a single chapter. But we find these descriptions of him to be clarifying as we make disciples. They are time-tested biblical truths, reflected in the rule of faith and creeds of the earliest Christians.[4]

1. JESUS IS BOTH FULLY HUMAN AND FULLY GOD

The Bible teaches it and the early Christians took a strong stand for it: Jesus is both 100 percent human and 100 percent divine. This is a profound mystery! The eternal Son of God became a human being named Jesus, born to a young Jewish woman, and raised in a small town in Israel. The Bible indicates that Jesus was self-limited in several ways during his time on earth, embracing the weaknesses that all humans experience—fear, loneliness, frustration, fatigue, temptation, physical pain. But the Bible is clear that despite some self-imposed limitations, Jesus was both fully human *and* fully God (see Col. 2:9 and Phil. 2:6–11).

John, one of Jesus' closest disciples, starts his gospel by telling us about the identity and origin of Jesus Christ. He tells us that Jesus was the Word and that the Word was God:

In the beginning was the Word, and the Word was with God, and the Word was God. He was with God in the beginning. Through him all things were made; without him nothing was made that has been made (John 1:1–3).

The Word became flesh and made his dwelling among us. We have seen his glory, the glory of the one and only Son, who came from the Father, full of grace and truth (John 1:14).

No one has ever seen God [the Father], but the one and only Son, who is himself God and is in closest relationship with the Father, has made him known (John 1:18).

John says that Jesus was the en-flesh-ment ("incarnation") of God. God became en-fleshed in a human man, and yet this man was also the Son of God, the Creator of heaven and earth—God in the flesh.[5] John is clear that the Word is the One through whom all things were made and that he is God.

> Jesus doesn't just give us truths; he is the truth. Jesus is the prophet to end all prophets. He gives us hard-copy words from God, truths on which we can build our lives, truths we have to submit to, truths we have to obey, and truths we have to build our lives on, but he himself is the truth.
>
> —TIM KELLER

The writer of Hebrews also makes sure that we know that Jesus was fully human:

Since the children have flesh and blood, he too [Jesus] shared in their humanity so that by his death he might break the power of him who holds the power of death—that is, the devil. . . . For this reason he had to be made like them, fully human in every way, in order that he might become a merciful and faithful high priest in service to God, and that he might make atonement for the sins of the people (Heb. 2:14–17).

This is why the virgin birth of Jesus is so important, not a secondary or optional doctrine of our faith as Christians. Mary gave birth to Jesus as her human son. Yet when Jesus was born, the angel called him "Immanuel," which means "God with us" (Matt. 1:23). Jesus has two natures—one fully human and one fully divine—yet they are united in a single person.

Why does any of this matter for discipleship? Here are some of the implications of this for being a disciple who makes disciples.

- As a human being, Jesus identifies with us, and we can identify with him (he is one of us). He can represent us as our substitute and our advocate before God the Father.
- As God, Jesus is worthy of our worship. He is the "son of man" seen by Daniel (7:13) and, in the book of Revelation, the one seated on God's throne and designated by God to judge the world. We can surrender to him and worship him (John 9:38).
- Since he was both fully human and fully divine, we can confidently imitate him and form our lives around him, knowing that the way he lived is the perfect example to us of a human life that honors God.
- Jesus wasn't immune from the sin in this world. Though he himself was blameless and without sin, he suffered the consequences of others' sin, and he shows us how to face temptation and death.
- Jesus shows us what love is. His love is pure and holy, given freely in grace to those who do not deserve it. We know

what love is because he first loved us. His love led him to seek and save the lost and make disciples.

- Jesus is the Word of God, and the Bible says that in him all things hold together. Everything exists because of him and everything exists for him. We can ask others to follow him because he is the wisest and most brilliant teacher who ever lived, and it is only in knowing him that our lives find their full meaning and purpose (Col. 2:3–9).

> The word *disciple* designates a learner or follower such as an apprentice. It always implies a personal attachment which shapes the whole of the disciple's life. It is the task of the disciple to learn, study, and pass along the sayings and teachings of the master.
>
> **—ROBERT COLEMAN**

Sometimes we fail to keep Jesus' identity as human and divine in balance, and a lack of emphasis one way or the other can hinder our ability to be true disciples who form our lives around him. Holding to the paradox of his dual nature ensures the proper role of Jesus in your life and in the lives of those whom you will disciple.

2. JESUS IS THE MESSIAH

The word *Christ* is not Jesus' last name. In the first century, that kind of naming was accomplished by saying where someone was from or who their father was: "Jesus of Nazareth" or "Jesus, son of Joseph." Instead, Christ is a title (like calling someone a teacher or a doctor) that also means "Messiah." So when we say "Jesus Christ," we are describing his identity: "He is Jesus *the Messiah.*"

But what does it mean to be "the Messiah"? Well, that requires some background. You can't understand what it means to call someone "the Hero" of the story unless you understand the story, who the characters are, what the danger is, and what it will take to win the day. So the only way to truly understand what it means to say Jesus is the Messiah is to understand the "Grand Story" of the Bible. This is something we should continue to read, study, and learn our entire lives as disciples, but here is a very brief introduction to the big plot points.

Creation: The Bible begins with God calling all things into being. Every part of creation is declared "good" by the Creator. God's creative work climaxes in his creation of human beings, uniquely made in his image to rule the world as his representatives. The first human beings, Adam and Eve, enjoyed warm and close fellowship with God in the garden of Eden.

Fall: God is both holy and loving. We were created to glorify him and to have an intimate relationship with him. Tragically, Adam and Eve were deceived by Satan and chose to rebel against God. By their decision, human beings are now spiritually dead and separated from God. We are incapable of undoing the effects of sin; we need God's saving intervention.

Covenant: God reached out to sinful humanity in several ways. He saved a man named Noah and his family in a time of judgment, making a covenant with him not to destroy the earth again in a flood. Then he offered a covenant to a man named Abraham that became an outline of his redemption plan in history. God promised to create a nation from Abraham and to bless all people of the world through him. Abraham believed God and accepted God's covenant, and God made Abraham's descendants into twelve tribes who became slaves in Egypt.

Israel: The story of the Bible continues with the descendants of Abraham, and we see how God, using Moses, liberates the twelve tribes from bondage in Egypt. God gave the Ten Commandments and the Law as a gift of grace, sacrifices for sin, and a special promised land to the tribes. God found in David, one of their kings, a faith so pleasing that God made another promise to fulfill his commitment to bless all people. He said that one of David's descendants would become the messianic King. His kingdom would never end and would be a paradise for God's people. The Messiah would also judge those outside his kingdom.

Jesus: Jesus came as this Messiah, our king, and in him, the kingdom of God broke into this sinful world. Jesus came to reveal the true nature of God and to restore and redeem God's original intent for humanity. Jesus' mission led him to the cross, where he suffered and died to save all people, both the Jews and the Gentiles (those not physically descended from Abraham). After three days Jesus rose from the dead, freeing us from Satan, and then he ascended into heaven. He is coming back again to fully restore God's kingdom. By repentance and faith in Jesus and his finished work on the cross, we can enter into his kingdom reign. He takes our sin away, he gives us the gift of the Holy Spirit, and we are adopted into his Father's family. Our old identity is dead, and we are a new creation through the grace of God, by faith in Jesus and what Jesus has done for us. We now live a new life, trusting and following him, as his disciples. This teaching is called the gospel, which means the good news. It is the best news anyone can ever hear!

Church: Before Jesus ascended into heaven, he gave his apostles a commission to carry on his teachings and make disciples. After ascending to heaven and taking his seat on God's throne, he sent the Holy Spirit and established a global community for those who placed their faith in him. Jesus is the head of this body, and he calls those in his church to use the gifts and the message he has given them to be disciples who make disciples. Disciples are people who love God and others and who live out God's kingdom reign in word and deed by reaching out to those who do not know the gospel and by showing compassion toward the poor and the oppressed. The life and teachings of Jesus form the blueprint for the mission and identity of the church, and the Holy Spirit unites disciples from different cultures, places, and times into one body—the body of Christ.

Restoration: Jesus promised his followers that he will return one day to fully remove the effects of the curse and usher in the new age to come where sin, death, pain, and sadness are gone forever. This is the blessed hope for all disciples of Jesus. Until that time, Jesus offers humans a standing invitation into his "already, but not yet kingdom." He offers salvation to us by grace through faith. Grace is God's unearned favor where he offers us forgiveness and life in his kingdom, and we respond to his offer by faith, which is trusting and following Jesus. When Jesus comes back, he will judge those living as well as those who have died. Those who did not respond to God's gracious invitation to be redeemed in this life will be punished for their sins in hell. Those who trusted and followed Jesus will experience everlasting joy with God forever in the new heaven and new earth.

These plot points are the major movements of God's story, but the key to understanding Jesus *as Messiah* is seeing how God's relationship with humanity is traced out in both the Old and New Testaments.[6] Every book in the Bible points to Jesus. Since Jesus came to lead us into a life as his disciples, not just to conversion, this story line is essential knowledge for disciple makers. You can only fully understand and follow who Jesus is and what he calls us into in light of this grand story.[7]

It answers all of the important questions for life.

- Did God make the world this way?
- What went wrong? Why is there such evil in this world?
- Why is the Old Testament important? What do the laws and stories mean?
- Why did Jesus have to die?
- What does God promise us?
- What is God's kingdom?
- Where is life going?
- What does all of this mean for me?

Answering these questions requires that we draw upon the full story of the Bible, including Jesus' work on the cross and his life story from the Gospels. The Messiah's identity is old, deep, and wonderfully complex, grounded in the Old Testament and made clear in the New.

> You are more sinful than you ever dared believe; you're more loved than you ever dared hope.
>
> —TIM KELLER

3. JESUS' GOSPEL IS OUR MESSAGE

The word *gospel* is an important word to know as you embark on the discipleship lifestyle. It literally means "good news." The gospel is, in the big picture, the story line of the Bible that we outlined for you above. But more narrowly, the Bible speaks of this good news as the announcement that Jesus has overcome the curse and the consequences of sin through his life, death on the cross, resurrection from the dead, and enthronement at the right hand of the Father. His work is the sole basis by which our sins can now be forgiven and we can be made right with God. His promised gift is the Holy Spirit, who enables our adoption into God's family and our empowerment for ministry. We respond with faith to these promises and to this amazing good news!

The gospel is good news because Jesus and his resurrection changed everything for every human being.[8] The key to understanding the gospel is recognizing that we live in an in-between time. We live between Jesus' first coming, where he died for our sins, was raised from the dead, and ascended into heaven, and his second coming, when he returns to judge the living and the dead and establish his kingdom, as the Old Testament promised.

In 1 Corinthians 15:1–6, as he prepares to give us the gospel in summary form, the apostle Paul highlights several of the benefits of the gospel for us:

> Now I would remind you, brothers, of the gospel I preached to you, which you received, in which you stand, and by which you are being saved, if you hold fast to the word I preached to you—unless you believed in vain. For I delivered to you as of first importance what I also received (ESV).

Paul's language is clear—believing, receiving, and standing in the gospel that has been preached to us saves us! Jesus and his work on the cross is the basis of our standing with God, and there is nothing more important! The passage goes on to summarize the core events of the gospel announcement:

> Christ died for our sins in accordance with the Scriptures, that he was buried, that he was raised on the third day in accordance with the Scriptures, and that he appeared to Cephas, then to the twelve. Then he appeared to more than five hundred brothers at one time, most of whom are still alive, though some have fallen asleep (ESV).

The gospel focuses on Jesus the Messiah's death for our sin. But the full gospel is not just his death; it includes his burial, resurrection, and appearances to his followers—*and how all of this happened in accordance with the broader story of Scripture.* Our response to the good news about what Jesus has done for us is to place our faith in him, to receive it as God's grace, God's gift to us.

Our friend Bill Hull describes what he calls the gospel elevator speech.[9] He encourages every disciple to study the Scriptures and to develop a brief description of the gospel that you could give to someone who asks you to summarize your faith as you ride up on an elevator with them. Disciple makers need to be clear about this. What's your gospel elevator speech? You need to know the gospel and help to ensure that those you disciple are clear on it too.

We believe there are five key parts to a good gospel elevator speech. We've summarized what he says with these five topics:

- Jesus' identity—that he is the Messiah and the Son of God.

- Jesus' work—what he did for us by his death for our sins and resurrection from the dead.
- Jesus' invitation—what he offers to us and how we respond by faith.
- Jesus' kingship—what responding to Jesus means for our lives here and now.
- Jesus' future promise—what it means for our lives when we die.

Here is our gospel elevator speech:

God sent Jesus—his only Son and our Messiah—into the world. He came to rescue us from the tragic consequences of our sin and show us how to live with God. He died and rose again as a sacrifice for our sins. He then ascended into heaven, where he rules and reigns until his return, giving us the gift of the Holy Spirit. God offers us forgiveness and a new life in his kingdom, but only if we will place our faith in Jesus. Those with active faith in Jesus are the true disciples of Jesus. Disciples follow Jesus, are changed by Jesus, and join the mission of Jesus. He is coming back and will judge the living and the dead, bringing his true disciples into paradise for a life of joy that will never end.

> Jesus has not given us options to consider. He has given us commands to obey.
>
> —DAVID PLATT

We tell people that when they are ready to believe this gospel as the defining story of their life, they are ready to become Christians and disciples of Jesus.

4. JESUS SAVES BY GRACE

Grace is another important word. The grace of God saves sinners. In grace, God gives us the free and unmerited gift of Jesus, whose life and death establish our right standing with God and save us from the eternal consequences of sin. The Bible teaches that we can only get right with God because of Jesus and the good news of what he has done. By grace, we are free to receive God's offer of forgiveness and place our faith in Jesus. God does not accept us because we are good people or because we do the right religious things. He offers us forgiveness freely, and we receive it as we place our lives, our future, and all of our hopes in his Son. When we rely on God's grace, looking away from ourselves in faith, God is pleased.

The best known statement on Jesus' grace is found in John 3:16–17:

> For God so loved the world that he gave his one and only Son, that whoever believes in him shall not perish but have eternal life. For God did not send his Son into the world to condemn the world, but to save the world through him.

God gives his grace to all who place their faith in Jesus. By his Spirit, God leads us to Jesus (1 John 2:20, 27; John 16:7–11), and we must respond with faith. Faith is more than an intellectual agreement with facts. It is a warm, heartfelt trust and commitment to Jesus, who he is and what he has done for us. The Bible describes how this "by grace . . . through faith" formula works for us in Ephesians 2:8–10.

> For it is by grace you have been saved, through faith—and this not from yourselves, it is the gift of God—not by works, so that no one can boast. For we are God's handiwork, created in Christ Jesus to do good works, which God prepared in advance for us to do.

This passage is clear that we are not saved by our works. But as we trust and follow Jesus, relying on his gift of salvation, the Bible tells us that we will begin to do what God created us to do—good works. God initiates this work by drawing us to himself. We respond in faith and our transformed lives produce the fruit of good works. A. T. Robertson, an expert on New Testament Greek, described it succinctly: "Grace is God's part, faith ours."[10] God initiates and draws us, we respond with faith, and the result is good works.

PAUSE AND PONDER

How does grace ignite love and obedience? Think of how this looks between parents and children, teachers and students, and especially Jesus and us.

In the book *Bono: In Conversation with Michka Assayas,* U2's Bono does a great job describing God's grace. After describing how the concept of karma is central to many religions, Bono explains how karma radically differs from the Christian understanding of grace.

> What you put out comes back to you: an eye for an eye, a tooth for a tooth, or in physics—in physical laws—every action

is met by an equal or an opposite one. It's clear to me that karma is at the very heart of the universe. I'm absolutely sure of it. And yet, along comes this idea called grace to upend all that "as you reap, so you will sow" stuff. Grace defies reason and logic. Love interrupts, if you like, the consequences of your actions, which in my case is very good news indeed, because I've done a lot of stupid stuff. . . . It doesn't excuse my mistakes, but I'm holding out for grace. I'm holding out that Jesus took my sins onto the cross, because I know who I am, and I hope I don't have to depend on my own religiosity.[11]

Indeed, something akin to karma is at work in the world. The Bible tells us that the law (summarized in the Ten Commandments) represents God's moral will for how we are to live. God's law reveals to us that our sinful acts require a moral response from God. But God's grace interrupts that "eye for an eye" response in an amazing way! At the cross, God's justice is fully satisfied by the sinless life of Jesus, and God's grace enables our forgiveness and the gift of the Holy Spirit. Grace is the foundation of the life of a disciple. We start in grace, and we are sustained by grace.

Discipleship is all about learning how to live a life grounded in Jesus' grace.

- We learn how Jesus forgives all our sins at conversion.
- We learn that Jesus and his cross are the grounds or basis of forgiveness.
- We learn to receive grace fresh every day in dependence on God's Spirit.
- We learn how God, in his grace, shows us new sins to confess.
- We learn to see how all of life is by God's grace.

---

5. SAVING FAITH IS FAITHFUL

As we've said before, saving faith is not just a mental assent to facts.[12] Faith includes facts, but it involves far more. It is living and alive. Faith is our response to God, a response that involves our head, heart, and hands. Faith is what leads a disciple to follow Jesus, be changed by Jesus, and join the kingdom mission of Jesus. Faith is God's work within us, a work that leads to good works that God prepared in advance for us to do (Eph. 2:10).

PAUSE AND PONDER

Did the concept of grace you were originally taught call for discipleship?

We put it this way: True faith is trusting and following Jesus. Both trust and obedience are essential.[13] The apostle James teaches us that faith without deeds is dead (James 2:26). As one writer put it: "Faith obeys. Un-belief rebels. The fruit of one's life reveals whether that person is a believer or an unbeliever. There is no middle ground. Merely knowing and affirming facts apart from obedience to the truth is not believing in the biblical sense."[14] In fact, in some contexts, the Greek word for faith (*pistis*) is best translated as *faithfulness*. Faith includes faithfulness, which means that we live with integrity, that we are trustworthy. It speaks of a life of obedience, one aimed away from sin and toward Jesus. Faith and faithfulness are the language of discipleship.[15]

There are many people today who have a false security and a false assurance that they have a "real relationship with God" when they do not by biblical standards. The most recent statistics show that 76 percent of Americans claim to be Christian.[16] But claiming faith is different from living out our faith as a true disciple. George Barna puts the problem this way: "Although most Americans consider themselves to be Christian and say they know the content of the Bible, less than one out of ten Americans demonstrate such knowledge through their actions."[17] The apostle John described it like this:

> We know that we have come to know him if we keep his commands. Whoever says, "I know him," but does not do what he commands is a liar, and the truth is not in that person (1 John 2:3–4).

True disciple makers are cognizant that many millions of people today are cultural Christians without true biblical faith. We say this not to condemn people or judge their sincerity, but because we love people and want to help them, as God guides to develop true faith.

One more important point. We do not place our faith in faith. We place our faith in Jesus. He is the ground and the object upon which we focus, even as he works within us and creates this faithful faith (Phil. 2:13). Our decisions to trust and follow him are the way God works through us to create this kind of faith (1 Cor. 15:1).

CULTURAL CHRISTIANITY	BIBLICAL FAITH
I like the things of Jesus being part of my life.	Jesus is at the center of my life.
I have a life and Jesus is in parts of it.	I form my life around Jesus.
I believe that Jesus was a good man/teacher.	I believe Jesus is Savior and Lord.
I was christened/made a one-time decision.	I trust and follow Jesus daily.
I pray to God when I need help.	I pray to God and seek his guidance daily.
God will save me; I am a good person.	God will save me; I have faith in Jesus.
God will forgive my sins because I am human.	God will forgive my sins because of Jesus.

6. SIN REMAINS IN THE MIDST OF SAVING FAITH

We are saved by grace through faith, and this is both an event (our justification) and a process (our sanctification). In other words, it *continues* from the time of our conversion to the end of our lives. The grace that made us right with God is the same grace that keeps us right with God. While we are saved from the eternal consequences of our sin, our daily battle against our sin has just begun! After conversion, disciples need to learn *how* to deal with sin.

In the Bible, the word *walk* is a common metaphor for the "basic direction of one's life." So a person with faith in Jesus "walks in the way of Jesus" or "walks in the light." One of the most helpful passages for dealing with sin is 1 John 1:5–9:

God is light; in him there is no darkness at all. If we claim to have fellowship with him and yet walk in darkness, we lie and do not live out the truth. But if we walk in the light, as he is in the light, we have fellowship with one another, and the blood of Jesus, his Son, purifies us from all sin. If we claim to be without sin, we deceive ourselves and the truth is not in us. If we confess our sins, he is faithful and just and will forgive us our sins and purify us from all unrighteousness.

There are three teachings in this passage that help disciples cling to God's grace by faith.

First, this passage tells us that those with true faith will still struggle with sin. We will fall short. As James puts it, "We all stumble in many ways" (3:2). John says in the passage above that if anyone claims to be without sin, Jesus' truth is not in that person (1:8). So we need to admit that sin is still a reality in our lives, and this real-life condition needs to be acknowledged and addressed, especially by disciple makers and church leaders. When we show transparency in speaking about our own struggle with sin, it helps those following us to realize that struggling with sin is a normal aspect of the Christian life.

I (Bobby) remember my early days as a new believer when I was discipled by my French professor and he shared some of his sin struggles with me. He talked about his pride and his battle against lust. One day we were in a store, and there was a magazine on the stand with a picture of a woman who was known for her nude scenes in movies. I started to say something negative in judgment about her, but Mac stopped me. "I would say the same thing, but I have found myself trapped in my own sinful and lustful thoughts far too often to be comfortable pointing my finger at others," he said. His awareness of his own weakness and sin gave him a humility toward others, and his example in this area was a concrete example of what it means to first take the plank out of my own eye before pointing out a speck in another's.

The second teaching we see in the passage from John's letter is that Jesus' blood provides ongoing forgiveness throughout life. Grace isn't a one-time event. It continues with us, always. In fact, it is evidence of God's grace that we grow in our awareness of our sin, leading to conviction. When this happens, we simply confess it, agreeing with God that sin is evil and choosing to prefer God rather than condone the fading pleasure of sin. And God forgives us.

Disciple makers may need to help their disciples learn how to do this as a regular habit in their lives and how to recover from significant falls into sin. John tells us that Jesus' blood cleanses us from ALL unrighteousness (1 John 1:9). This means every sin you can imagine. Our confession is a sign that we hate and reject our sin, and we need a Savior who is greater than our sin. God often uses other disciples to help and encourage us in this battle to overcome sin in our lives (Heb. 3:12–13). James says, "Confess your sins to each other and pray for each other so that you may be healed" (James 5:16).

The third takeaway from John's letter is that struggling with sin is different than giving in to a lifestyle of sin. If we purposefully and willfully embrace sinful lifestyles, we show that we are not in agreement with God about our sin. If we consistently love our sin, preferring it to God or justifying our sin as something that God does not hate or judge, then there is a problem with our faith. Hebrews 10:26 warns us if we "deliberately keep on sinning." These ongoing sinful patterns are inconsistent with true faith, and if not addressed, over time can lead us into a place where our faith is shown to be dead or, some believe, becomes dead, nonexistent. First John tells us that we do not live by Jesus' truth when we "walk" or willfully live in the darkness of sinful lifestyle patterns. This is an alarming situation for disciples and disciple makers. Biblical faith is alive. It is an active and repentant faith, present from the beginning of our relationship with Jesus until the end of our lives.

> If Jesus rose from the dead, then you have to accept all that he said; if he didn't rise from the dead, then why worry about any of what he said? The issue on which everything hangs is not whether or not you like his teaching, but whether or not he rose from the dead.
>
> —TIM KELLER

LET'S GET INTO THE WHEELBARROW ...

About 150 years ago, a man named Charles Blondin came to the United States from overseas. He was fascinated by the Niagara Falls, and he resolved that he would walk over them on a tightrope. So he made a hemp cord 1,100 feet across, 160 feet above Niagara Falls, and announced he was going to cross from one side to the other. He was quite a showman, and after his announcement, a crowd of 100,000 gathered to watch him walk a tightrope across Niagara Falls, inch-by-inch, step-by-step. Can you imagine what it would be like to experience that moment?

Remember that this is life or death. There is no safety net. Charles crossed over successfully on his first attempt! Many people, of course, were taking pictures of him, so he did it again. This time he brought a camera with him and took a picture of the crowd while they were taking pictures of him. Then he went a third time and took a chair along. He even balanced the chair on the rope and then stood on the chair. He went back a fourth time and made an omelet, lowering it down to the passengers on the *Maid of the Mist* (a boat in the river below) so that one of them could have it for breakfast. Another time he took a wheelbarrow along with him. The crowd went crazy.

After he returned with the wheelbarrow, Charles turned to the crowd and asked them, "Do you believe I can cross again?" Of course, they all shouted that they believed him. But then he asked them a different, but related, question: "Now . . . who will get into the wheelbarrow?"

Suddenly, it got really quiet.

All 100,000 observers were silent. Then a man named Harry Colcord spoke up. He knew Blondin and had worked with him before. He got into the wheelbarrow—inch-by-inch . . . step-by-step. Can you imagine that ride? In a wheelbarrow, on a tightrope, crossing over Niagara Falls. Good news. They made it to the other side.

Jesus never went up to people and said, "Admire me." He wasn't looking for people to affirm him from a distance. No, he offered invitations. He made it personal. "Trust and follow me," he said. "Whoever wants to be my disciple must deny themselves and take up their cross and follow me" (Matt. 16:24).

In other words, "Get in the wheelbarrow and let me lead you."

FOR REFLECTION AND CONVERSATION

1. What is the connection between Jesus' nature and our willingness to trust and follow him? How does it help us to know that he was fully human and fully God?

2. Why is the bigger story of God so vital to understanding Jesus and his cross?

3. In what ways does a person's understanding of Jesus and his gospel impact the kind of disciple they become?

4. What do you think about the contrast between being a biblical disciple or a cultural Christian? How does a proper understanding of Jesus impact this contrast?

5. How can the simple definition of disciple making as "helping people trust and follow Jesus" help you as you make disciples?

Chapter 6

INTENTIONALITY

> "Physical training is good, but training for godliness
> is much better, promising benefits in this life
> and in the life to come." This is a trustworthy
> saying, and everyone should accept it.
> 1 TIMOTHY 4:8–9 (NLT)

The *Oxford English Dictionary* describes intentionality as "the fact of being deliberate or purposive" (yes, *purposive* is a word!).[1] Intentionality is a key element of the disciple-making process because all discipleship has a purpose, a goal, and a plan to reach that goal. Disciple makers know where other people need to go, and they have a plan to help them get there.

There is a tendency in some spiritual circles to celebrate humility in a way that minimizes the importance of planning and strategy. Our postmodern culture does not like those who use pat answers and oversimplified methods. Nor do we like those who talk and act as if they might know the way. We are suspicious of those who claim knowledge or insight about a spiritual journey for others. The world pushes away from absolutes. Instead, we prize the modesty of uncertainty and admire self-professed expressions of doubt. Even among Christians, there is a common posture that people take, saying, "Only God can guide people." "Our only job," they say, "is to pray and trust the Holy Spirit's guidance in another person's life."[2]

> To become a disciple of Jesus requires intentionality—a purposeful attempt to foster the discipleship process day in and day out.
>
> —RICHARD FOSTER

We understand that some have concerns about making discipleship too programmed or rigid or not organic. And we know that groups in the past that emphasized disciple making utilized power and control tactics. But the pendulum may have swung too far in the other direction. We believe it is important for the church today to recover models for discipleship that are intentional, based on the example of Jesus. Let's look at a concrete example of what we're talking about. I (Bobby) have been very strategic with a men's group I started. I wanted to make sure that I had the right men and that I was discipling them in a way that would have a lasting impact. Here are four *intentional* choices I made to make this happen:

1. I *intentionally* picked a small number of men for the group.
2. I *intentionally* asked those I selected to commit to a group covenant and made the expectations for belonging to the group clear. I was clear in communicating that they should join the group only if they were going to uphold the agreement, and it was *okay* to say no if they weren't ready.
3. I *intentionally* selected the material for us to use, books and studies that are easily reproduced so the men could take what they learned and use it with others.
4. I *intentionally* asked one of the men in the group to be my apprentice. He was responsible for leading the group when I could not attend. This experience was to prepare him to lead his own group after we are finished with our group time.

I had these intentions for the group from the beginning, which meant that I had to be selective and narrow my focus in making decisions. It meant that there were men I wanted to be in the group but could not invite because they weren't able to meet some or all of the criteria I had set.

Some people may feel that I was controlling or rigid in my criteria for the group. But that denies the essence of being intentional—it means that you must be selective. In saying "yes" to some things, you must say "no" to others. In my experience (and as I've talked to discipleship leaders around the nation), I've found that being selective and intentional can make for a highly effective group experience. Josh and I have both launched and facilitated dozens of discipling communities over the years, and without exception the groups with an intentional leader have actually been *more* vibrant and free than the groups that adopt an "anything goes" mentality.

Nonintentionality over time does not work. Being organic is good, but if we are organic and without a good plan, it will lead nowhere. Sometimes Jesus is characterized as a free-spirited, homeless vagabond living out of a trash can, floating from town to town with no real plan—a guru who spoke in Hallmark platitudes, told some stories, and performed good works for the poor. Seriously? This is not the real Jesus of the Bible. Jesus always had a purpose in what he did.

> Since making disciples is the main task of the church, every church ought to be able to answer two questions: What is our plan for making disciples of Jesus? Is our plan working?
>
> —DALLAS WILLARD

But don't take our word for it. Let's examine a few sections of Scripture. One is from the New Testament and the other comes from the Old Testament. The best-known text on discipleship in the New Testament is Jesus' words in Matthew 28:19–20. As you read it, take note of anything that speaks of having a purpose or a goal, an objective that Jesus wants his disciples to accomplish.

> "Therefore go and make disciples of all nations, baptizing them in the name of the Father and of the Son and of the Holy Spirit, and teaching them to obey everything I have commanded you. And surely I am with you always, to the very end of the age."

This text has a clear command: "make disciples." We can only "make disciples" if we know *what* a disciple is and *how* to make one. In other words, Jesus gives us a clear objective. And to reach that objective requires a strategy and a plan. By definition, a disciple maker is guided by intentionality and planning.

That's not to say that it's all up to us, that the success of God's mission and his plans for this world are entirely dependent on our best efforts. Thank God! There is a balance here. Notice that after giving commands for his disciples to accomplish, the text ends with a promise of Jesus' presence (by his Spirit). Jesus tells us that in the disciple-making process, he is with us always, even to the very end of the age. So we do our part—obeying what he commands and strategically planning how to accomplish what he gives us to do—and we trust that Jesus is working in us and through us to make what we cannot do on our own happen through those efforts.

> In order to grow up spiritually, we need to deliberately make space in our lives for God. Like any relationship, our connection with God will atrophy and become unhealthy if not nurtured.
>
> —DALLAS WILLARD

I make disciples (as Jesus commanded me to do), but I do not do it by myself. I do not just leave it all up to Jesus either, and that's not unspiritual or wrong. It's simply doing what Jesus has asked me to do. He has commanded me to do my part, *and he expects me to do it.* He has promised that he will be with me and works through me as I do what he asks. We need an actionable plan because, according to the text, making disciples includes my role in teaching them "to obey everything that Jesus commanded."[3] My job is to be intentional in teaching disciples about Jesus.

There are three activities involved in discipleship. There is my activity as the disciple maker. There is God's activity by his Spirit and through his Word. And there is the disciple's activity as he or she responds to the direction of both the disciple maker and the Holy Spirit. If I lack a strategy or I'm not sure what it means to make a disciple or what a disciple looks like— well, I probably won't make disciples. And if my plan isn't aligned with Jesus and what he is doing through the Holy Spirit, it won't make disciples either.

Jesus did not tell us that the Holy Spirit would make disciples. He gave that order to us, and that means we must learn how to partner with the Holy Spirit in order to do it. *The fact remains—discipleship is a mission that's ultimately been assigned to us.* We are responsible to do our part. Just read the text. As the old-time preachers said, "It says what it says."

We mentioned that we see this focus on intentionality in the Old Testament as well. The passage we're looking at in the Old Testament is slightly different, but has a similar focus on being intentional. It's God's guidance for Israelite parents in raising their children to know the Lord. Deuteronomy 6 provides clear direction for parents on discipling their children. You could call it the Great Commission *before* the Great Commission. In these few short verses, God uses Moses to succinctly describe the heart of disciple making. And though the context is speaking to parents and children, the principles apply in all discipling relationships. Jesus modeled what Moses teaches in these verses with his own disciples.

These verses begin with what is often called the *Shema* (pronounced *SKE-ma* or *sh'ma*), which in Hebrew means "hear."[4] As you read the passage, notice the emphasis on life-on-life teaching of the truth about God through the rhythms of everyday life:

> "Hear, O Israel: The LORD our God, the LORD is one. Love the LORD your God with all your heart and with all your soul and with all your strength. These commandments that I give you today are to be on your hearts. Impress them on your children. Talk about them when you sit at home and when you walk along the road, when you lie down and when you get up. Tie them as symbols on your hands and bind them on your foreheads. Write them on the doorframes of your houses and on your gates" (Deut. 6:4–9).

Did you notice any intentionality? "Impress" God's commandments upon your children. "Talk" about God's commandments when you "sit," when you "walk," when you "lie down," and when you "get up." These aren't optional suggestions. They are commands to be mindful and focused. I (Bobby) was so impressed with this model of discipleship that I coauthored a book called *Dedicated: Training Your Children to Trust and Follow Jesus* to assist parents with intentional relational discipleship in raising their children to follow Jesus.[5] This passage describes how Israelite parents were to help their children learn and think about God's commands, to "meditate on them, so that their obedience would not be a matter of formal legalism, but a response based upon understanding."[6]

The method prescribed for parents in the Old Testament is almost identical to the method Jesus used with his disciples. Jesus did most of his teaching with his disciples in the context of real life. Jesus taught as they walked along the road, while they were doing ministry, before they would lie down for the night. He taught in the context of conflict with religious leaders and in response to questions from the crowd. Jesus was flexible in his program, but highly intentional as well.

> If we do not make the journey from theories and ideals to concrete situations, then the concrete situations will be lost under a smog of words.
>
> **—ROBERT COLEMAN**

This intentionality is seen in his selection of the twelve disciples and especially the three key leaders (Peter, James, and John).[7] While he taught the crowds, he also held back some of his teaching and shared it exclusively with his disciples. Jesus was disciplined, a man of prayer who prioritized his time with his Father so that he could respond to the events of the day, knowing that the Father had prepared them for him. And if we are thoughtful and prayerful, we can apply many of these same practices today.

> Participating with God means knowing what part is our part, and what part is God's part. If we try to do too much of the work, we fall into a religion of self-effort that will fail to transform our inner life. If we do too little and just wait for God to take over our lives and fix everything, we do not learn the tasks necessary to mature spiritually, and again nothing changes. Our real job is to submit to the task of learning, and to become His apprentices of life and love.
>
> —DALLAS WILLARD

Intentionality and planning do not mean that we are rigid or that we always have everything figured out. All disciple makers make mistakes. And our God-honoring efforts are far more important than having excellent strategies. For example, I (Bobby) have been in a discipling relationship with a younger man for a few years. I look back and I see many of the mistakes that I made, times when I didn't have a clear direction for our times together, sometimes asking the wrong men to join us. We went through a lot of ups and downs together, and I wish that I knew then (when we started) what I know now. But God still used our relationship for great good.

In the end, we make our plans and give them to the Lord, and he guides our steps. You can never predict if someone in your group will experience loss or sickness or a key life transition. There will always be hidden secrets or things you didn't know or plan for that come up in your relationships. But God works through these circumstances. My friend has recounted for me on a few occasions the things he has learned, and more often than not the things that stand out to him are not the ones I had on our agenda.

- How to handle death (he watched me deal with my younger sister's sudden death).
- How to deal with staff problems (he watched me deal with the church staff).
- How to deal with people in other religions (a conversation we had that deeply impacted the way his whole family now approaches this topic).

At the same time, he did learn several important things that I intentionally taught him.

- How to lead his daughter to commit her life to Christ in baptism.
- How to teach his nonbelieving brother-in-law the gospel by both his words and actions.
- How to be in relationship with and learn from older men.

Relationships like this one are real sources of joy in life. A few weeks ago, my friend called and left a message for me, thanking me for discipling him. He described what it meant to him personally, and it was such an encouraging voice mail that I kept it for weeks.

Am I saying that we should just pray and let God take care of the rest? No. This is *not* an excuse to throw out the agenda and fail to plan. But it's a recognition that our plans need to be adapted to God's purposes, something that we are continually learning to recognize as we grow in relationship with those we disciple. Our relationship is intentional, and we have a plan and a goal for our times together, but we are also flexible, adapting to changing circumstances and looking for those times when Jesus wants to teach us both something as we journey through life together.

1. YOU NEED A PLAN

Not too long ago several leaders in our church sat down with Randy Pope, the senior pastor of Perimeter Church in Atlanta. Perimeter is known throughout the world for effectively designing and implementing a life-on-life missional discipleship model throughout the church. Toward the end of the second day, Randy shared something with our group that is worth repeating here. "Too many pastors talk about disciple making but fail their people because they do not give them practical plans that enable them to do it," Randy said, adding that "it is essential to take disciple making from an abstract concept or theory into natural, simple practices." Randy knows what we've been talking about, something all disciple makers need: good plans!

You need to know where you are going with people and how you plan to get there. That plan should be basic and flexible, but it needs to have clear goals and strategies. If you don't have a plan or a strategy, you might want to start by talking to your church leaders. If you go to discipleship.org, we list various discipleship ministries with programs you can review to get started.

I (Bobby) recall spending some time at a conference with Steve Arterburn of New Life Ministries. New Life is an amazing Christian ministry that helps people with addictions or compulsive behaviors and equips them to deal with the hard challenges of life. Toward the end of the conference, Steve described the difference between Christians who overcome their addictions and those who do not. And what he taught us applies directly to being intentional in our disciple making. Steve said:

> People are often more than willing to repent and change. They will say all the right things and they mean it. The problem is not their intentions. The problem is their *lack of a commitment to a tried-and-true process* that works. If they do not commit to and stay with a proven strategy that deals with the underlying problem, they will not change by their best intentions.

Imagine you meet someone who has been an alcoholic for years. You meet up with him the day after he stops drinking, and he sincerely tells you that he is going to change. He has good intentions, but he lacks true intentionality—a plan to succeed. Would you bet a year's salary on him at that point? What if you met him after a thirty-day period in a rehab center? Would that change your bet? What if he had gone through a treatment center and he had been in Alcoholics Anonymous and was now sober for twenty-five years? Would that make you bet on his success?

If we want people to become disciples of Jesus, they need good discipleship plans and wise direction from disciple makers. Good intentions are not enough. Discipleship is more than just hanging out with people and having a good time.

- The Great Commission in Matthew 28:19–20 assumes that we will have a plan to "make disciples."
- Moses told parents to be very intentional about teaching their children God's commands.
- Those who are experts at helping people grow tell us that it requires a good plan.
- Jesus followed plans and had a master strategy.

2. YOU NEED TOOLS

Have you ever tried to build something without the right tools? Cutting 2x4 studs can take five minutes if you have a circular saw. If you don't, sawing them by hand takes time, and you are more likely to make mistakes or just give up. Tools make all the difference in helping you accomplish your goal. They give us practical, simple ways to actually do the work of making disciples. Without them, most of us will flounder because we are not trained or equipped like a pastor or someone with years of experience and several Bible degrees. If we're left to "figure it out" for ourselves, it's too difficult. We will give up.

Some disciple-making tools are very simple and easy to use. Ralph Moore started a movement of churches about forty years ago, and he has seen 2,300+ new churches planted out of the ones he planted. I (Bobby) asked Ralph how he was able to multiply and make disciple making so easy. "We invite people into relationships," he explained. "Then we invite them to our church gathering on Sunday where we preach one chapter from the Bible each week. From there, we have everyone get into a group in a home or coffee shop during the week, and each group follows the same format." Moore's groups don't have a complicated curriculum they follow. It's just three simple questions:

1. What did the Holy Spirit tell you during the teaching Sunday?
2. What are you doing about it?
3. How can we help you by our prayers and support?

They also provide additional training for small group leaders, who meet regularly with pastoral staff to work through leadership books and Scripture. But the format stays the same in these leadership huddles. They ask the same three questions they ask in small groups, applying those questions to their leadership readings. That's all they do. It's a simple tool.

Randy Pope takes a more in-depth approach, but he still works to make it something everyday Christians can do. The life-on-life model at Perimeter emphasizes curriculum and homework. Theology, Bible study, and doctrine are important to the church and the leadership, so they make it easily accessible but still an essential aspect of the material. Randy and his team have done a lot of work over the last twenty years to create a user-friendly curriculum. And they train all of their leaders in how to use it. The church has a high number of people in discipling relationships outside of Sunday mornings, intentionally following Jesus' method of disciple making. It's taken time and effort, but Perimeter leaders have cracked the code on making deeper theology both practical and learnable.

If you aren't sure where to begin, call on the leaders of your church to help you with the plan and the tools. It is everybody's job to grow to be disciples who make disciples, but it is not everybody's job to be a leader. Get help with tools from your leaders so you can be the best disciple maker possible.

As you look for tools to help you, remember the following:

- The most important tool is the Bible.
- People have always needed tools and aids to help them follow Jesus.
- Disciple makers can provide disciples with things like simple booklets.
- Disciple makers can utilize practical outlines.

> A mature disciple maker can point to several people he has discipled who are now discipling others.
>
> —JIM PUTMAN

3. YOU NEED TO BE A ROLE MODEL

One important aspect of intentionality is *imitation*. How do disciples learn? By watching those they learn from. And those who we disciple are watching us. Often, what we do will matter more than what we say. There is an old saying that applies here: "Who you are either amplifies or drowns out your words." An anonymous poem summarizes this well.

> The Gospels of Matthew, Mark, Luke, and John
> Are read by more than a few.
> But the one that is most read and commented on
> Is the gospel according to you.
> You are writing a gospel, a chapter each day,
> By the things that you do and the words that you say.[8]

The apostle Paul wrote in 1 Corinthians 4:15–17:

> I became your father through the gospel. Therefore I urge you to imitate me. For this reason I have sent to you Timothy, my son whom I love, who is faithful in

the Lord. He will remind you of my way of life in Christ Jesus, which agrees with what I teach everywhere in every church.

And the writer of Hebrews says much the same thing in 13:7:

Remember your leaders, who spoke the word of God to you. Consider the outcome of their way of life and imitate their faith.

We want to live lives that we want others to follow. A few years ago, I (Bobby) became friends with a man named William Lane who had recently moved to our community. I had known this man's name from my seminary days when I read some of his books. He was highly respected as a biblical scholar, and I thought it was wonderful that he had chosen to move into our community. He attended a weekly early-morning gathering of pastors and other Christian leaders in our community called the "empty hands" fellowship.

A few weeks after first meeting Lane, I learned that over the years he had discipled a well-known Christian song writer by the name of Michael Card (who also attended the meetings). Lane told me that he had moved to our town of Franklin because he had incurable cancer, and he had moved to be near to his friend Michael. He told me of a phone call he had with Michael before moving, where he said to him, "I want to come to Franklin . . . I want to show you how a Christian man dies."

The two men had a very close relationship, and Lane wanted to end his life helping Michael Card to become an even more seasoned disciple, someone who would influence other disciples. Lane soon died, and there was a huge celebration at his death. He left a wonderful legacy of commitment to Jesus and was an authentic example of a disciple of Christ.

We share this story to encourage you that as we point people to Jesus, we must also be aware of what they learn through our actions and words. We want to live out authentic lives as followers of Jesus so they can see him by our actions. And there are some very practical ways we can do this!

- We seek to treat our spouses and children well.
- We reveal what it means to follow Jesus through our use of social media.
- We speak well of others and uphold their honor, especially when they are not present.
- We watch what we eat and drink (not too much).
- We set an example in our devotional life and our church attendance.

> There is a beautiful transparency to honest disciples who never wear a false face and do not pretend to be anything but who they are.
>
> —BRENNAN MANNING

Remember that you will make mistakes and fail as a disciple. Our modelling of the Christian life is never perfect—only Jesus lived the perfect life, the true model we follow. Yet in our failure and sin we model what it means to live in the grace and mercy of God, to confess our sin and repent, to receive God's forgiveness, and to honor Christ through our honest dependence on him. You won't be sinless in your example, but you can model what it looks like to be a forgiven sinner walking in the grace of God!

4. YOU NEED TO BE DISCERNING

This may surprise some of you, but we believe that you should *not* disciple everyone who wants to be discipled by you. Many disciple-making efforts fail because they match the wrong people together in a discipling relationship. Here are a few examples of some of the things that can go wrong:

- Some people in the group do not want to study the Bible, so the whole group stops reading it.
- Some people are not as committed to meeting as regularly as others, so the group hardly meets.
- Some people have relational problems that get the group off track every time it meets.
- Some people do not keep confidentialities, so no one wants to personally share.
- Some people are ungodly, and they get the group off track.

Discipling groups gravitate to the lowest common denominator. So put the bar where you believe God wants it to be and stick with it. You will need a good, prayerful plan of action where you invite the people you have intentionally chosen into a discipling relationship with you. You want to be very selective about those you will invest your time in.

We highlighted this in an earlier chapter when we looked at the need to discern whom to select, but we want to unpack it in more detail for you here. At our church we teach our disciple makers to look for people who fit the "AFTeR" profile. You are looking for someone who matches the following:

- *Available.* They make themselves available for the things of God. This can include non-Christians who show an openness to God and to the gospel and may even be interested in reading and studying the Bible with you. You also want people who have the time or are willing to make the time to meet regularly.
- *Faithful.* They are faithful in attending the meeting. If you don't know them very well, you might ask them if there are any current or upcoming commitments that would affect their ability to meet for the time you have committed to meet. You can also involve other people in their decision. Josh, for example, asks the men he meets with to have their wives agree to the meeting time. This creates additional accountability and support at home. The people who are faithful will consistently follow through on what they've been asked to do.
- *Teachable.* They are receptive to guidance and instruction. They are humble in spirit and want to learn new things.
- *Reliable.* They have demonstrated a trustworthy character and consistently do what is asked.

When we look at leaders in the New Testament, we find that they followed a similar pattern of intentionally choosing people to train up and disciple as leaders. When Paul traveled, he shared the gospel freely, but he focused his attention on those who responded to his message. He focused on those who were interested, teachable, and committed to learning. There's much we can learn from the early church in selecting and training disciples today! Consider a few other examples:

- Jesus picked his twelve disciples only after many months of relationship with them and a night of prayer.
- The apostle Paul was discerning and careful of the way he invested himself.
- The apostle Paul taught Timothy to invest in reliable people who were capable of investing in others (2 Tim. 2:2).
- The Bible repeatedly warns us to avoid certain people (Proverbs).

Be selective. Notice that the criteria for selection do not include choosing your friends or people of certain personalities or who have other distinguishing qualities that make them different from you. Being selective means that you are discerning, but it is not an excuse to discriminate. The church of Jesus is a place where diverse people of all backgrounds, ethnicities, and personalities are united together. Some of the best discipling relationships are with people who are very different from you!

5. INTENTIONALITY IS THE KEY TO MULTIPLICATION AND REACHING PEOPLE

Before we close this chapter, we want to draw your attention to one key point. If you spend time around disciple makers, read the best disciple-making books, and study disciple making throughout church history, you will notice one common factor. Those who succeed are *intentional*. Intentionality is the single most important element, the one that separates those who multiply disciple makers from those who do not.

Many people try to make disciples. Most people make at least some attempt to disciple their children in the home, friends who come to know Jesus, or people who want to grow in their church. But intentionality is what distinguishes godly, committed disciples who are *not effective* at making disciples from godly, committed disciples who *are effective* at making disciples. You can grasp everything else we talk about in this book, but if you neglect the "Intentionality Principle," you will be hindered in reaching people, making disciples, and multiplying disciple makers.

When I (Josh) met Scott in spring 2003, it was obvious that he didn't trust or follow Jesus. His wife coerced him to attend one of our Easter worship gatherings. He was a new face in the crowd, so I approached him and asked some questions about his background. He described himself as "non-religious" and "skeptical" about the claims Jesus made about himself. I told him that I appreciated his candor and would like to hear more of his story. I was intentionally engaging with him in hopes that God would use me.

He didn't reject the idea of another conversation, so I invited him to lunch. That invitation was the start of weekly lunch meetings that continued for six months. Most of the time we talked about sports, marriage, and our careers . . . and sometimes we talked about Jesus. I gave up the time in my schedule to be with Scott because I knew that God was doing something here. I also understand that conversion is a process, and it often takes time to get to know someone. Scott needed me to invest this much in him to build trust and a good relationship.

Scott's curiosity in Jesus was piqued when *The Passion of the Christ* came out in theaters. After we saw the movie together, we unpacked the experience over a cup of coffee. After his third sip, Scott whipped out a five-page list of questions the movie had provoked. I answered the ones I knew and said "I don't know" to the ones I didn't. A few days later, I was led to intensify my prayers for Scott and his eternal destiny. In those prayers, I discerned God prompting me to invite Scott to join a small group of guys who met for encouragement and

Bible study each week. Much to my surprise, he was quite open to such an invitation. At this point Scott was now part of our intentional meeting plan, designed to help people grow.

This weekly immersion in Christian fellowship was exactly what Scott needed. It drew him like a moth to a flame to see the beauty and supremacy of Jesus. We didn't try to answer all of his questions. We had unanswered questions of our own! We just loved him, confessed our struggles, and walked with Scott and with each other for six months. Near the end of that time Scott began to talk in a way that indicated he believed that Jesus was the Son of God, his Lord and Messiah, that he had died for our sins and was raised to free us from death.

It began with a desire to reach him. I intentionally followed up with a plan. And God used all of this to reach Scott.

Eight years and two churches later, Scott called me out of the blue just to catch up. He told me that he had recently formed a discipleship group for men called a "Jesus group." He said that he was "paying it forward" and continuing the work I had done with him many years ago. I immediately went silent and felt my eyes tearing up. All I could say was, "Thank you, Jesus."

We have found that the single most pressing challenge to intentionality is the busyness of life. Most of the people in our church are trapped in this chaos—juggling the demands of a career, family, friends, church, hobbies (and kids' sports!), along with the multitude of needs presented by family members. Being intentional means that we *make time* for focused attention, and we do this persistently. It is not easy. We must apply our entire being to the task of engagement for a period of time, and then do it often enough to maintain some continuity so it becomes a habit and a discipline.

Intentionality is not a one-time decision. It is a decision that must be made every day. Here are some suggestions to help you get started:

- The first thing you want to do is learn an effective model from other disciple makers.
- Pray to God and ask him to guide you into an overall discipleship strategy for those you are discipling.
- Develop a schedule for the meeting, material to study (see the next chapter), and plan for relationship development.
- Determine that you will intentionally show the people that you are discipling your real life, warts and all. We have found that this is one of the most strategically helpful things. Paul and Jesus let their disciples see everything; they did not hold back. Shared real-life experiences provide some of the best examples that help disciples understand what it means for them to follow in your path.

FOR REFLECTION AND CONVERSATION

1. What is intentionality, and why is it important in discipleship? Review Matthew 28:19–20. In what ways do both "go" and "make disciples" require intentionality?

2. What is the intentionality process of Deuteronomy 6:4–9? How did parents apply it? How did Jesus apply it? How can you apply it?

3. What is the strategy Paul describes in 2 Timothy 2:2? How can you apply Paul's intentionality in your goals as you make disciples? What is your strategy?

4. Each discipling relationship requires specific knowledge and practical skills. For the discipling relationship you want, what special knowledge and skills do you need? If you do not have them, how can you acquire them?

Chapter 7

BIBLE

> All Scripture is God-breathed and is
> useful for teaching, rebuking, correcting
> and training in righteousness.
>
> 2 TIMOTHY 3:16

Years ago I (Bobby) worked during the summer for my father's company at my home in Calgary in Alberta, Canada, while I carried on a serious relationship with a young lady who lived in Memphis, Tennessee. We had met at college one year earlier. At that time phone calls were very expensive and email hadn't yet been invented, so we often wrote letters to each other to keep up the relationship. I would look forward to getting her letters when the mail arrived, and I read them carefully and enjoyed them very much. Even though this was over thirty years ago, I kept each one and still have them today.

When a new letter would arrive, I would open it and immediately read it over and over, several times in a row. These letters were my primary connection with this special lady. In reading her letters, I learned more and more about her. Through her letters, she was "present" to me even though we were physically separate and she was more than 2,000 miles away in Tennessee. I say that she was "present" because through her writings I learned things about her that I had not known, and this knowledge deepened our relationship. I better understood the things she liked, her opinions on issues, and learned things about her personality as well.

Through the relationship we developed, writing and reading letters, I came to love this woman. Three months later, when we were finally able to meet again in person, I had made up my mind. I asked her to marry me, and she became my wife four months later.

While there are some big differences between the letters I wrote to my wife and the Bible, there are some significant similarities to my experience with my wife and the way a Christian relates to God through the Bible. The Bible is a library of collected letters and writings. And while each letter is written by a human author and addressed to a specific historical context, there is also a single, divine author who is writing to his people, those who love him from different times, places, and circumstances.

The Bible is God's "letter" to us, and by reading the Bible, with all of the different genres and contexts, we can learn more and more about God. In a way that was not possible with my wife, God truly becomes present with us when we study his Word through the Holy Spirit. As we seek to know God through reading Scripture, we not only learn facts about

him—his likes, dislikes, opinions, motives, and personality—we actually interact with him and develop a relationship with him. The more we study God's Word, the more we come to know, experience, and love the author of that Word in deeper and deeper ways.

> Making disciples is all about seeing people transformed by the power of God's Word. If you want to see that happen in others, you need to be experiencing such transformation yourself.
>
> —FRANCIS CHAN

This practice of studying, reading, and meditating on God's Word is fundamental to what it means to be a disciple of Jesus. And growing as a disciple who knows and loves God is the ultimate purpose and meaning behind the Bible—why it was written. God created the Bible as his inspired and authoritative Word because its teachings are the primary means by which we develop a relationship with him.

The purpose of the Bible is to unveil the identity and the greatness of Jesus. Every book, chapter, and verse is there to clarify, reveal, or underscore something about Jesus. This is why the Bible is a key resource for making disciples. We need to use it wisely and with prayer to equip the people we're investing in so they meet Jesus as they read the Word.

In discipleship, we commit ourselves to learning how to live as Jesus would live if he were in our place. This means that discipleship is first and foremost about walking with God in everyday life. Are we truly *following* Jesus, being *changed* by Jesus, and *committed to the mission* of Jesus? A common mistake is to think of discipleship as mastering the content of the Bible, equating discipleship with education or memorization. While learning facts and memorizing Scripture can be good and helpful, they are not the goal. The focus of discipleship is knowing Jesus and trusting and following him in everyday life.

> The Bible is the means through which we are introduced to Jesus and invited to follow Him.
>
> —RICHARD FOSTER

Other people make the opposite mistake. They think the Bible is optional, or they are intimidated by the idea of studying and memorizing, and they distance themselves from study because it is too hard or difficult. But no one promised that being a disciple would be easy! Discipleship requires a commitment to learn about Jesus and his ways. Jesus' lordship is expressed when we carefully follow the teachings of the Bible, and we can't follow what we don't know! The apostle Paul described a key aspect of discipleship—taking our thoughts captive in obedience to Christ—in 2 Corinthians 10:5:

> We demolish arguments and every pretension that sets itself up against the knowledge of God, and we take captive every thought to make it obedient to Christ.

If obedience to Jesus Christ is our goal, then it will require a certain way of thinking. In Romans 12:2, the apostle Paul wrote:

> Do not conform to the pattern of this world, but be transformed by the renewing of your mind. Then you will be able to test and approve what God's will is—his good, pleasing and perfect will.

Transformation, Paul says, is first grounded in "the renewing of [the] mind." So while knowledge is not the end goal of discipleship, it is vitally important! How we think will determine how we live. It's impossible to overstate how important it is to get people into the Bible.[1]

Discipleship requires a manual, and the manual for learning to be a follower of Jesus is the Bible. Second Timothy 3:16–17 describes the role Scripture should play in the life of a disciple:

> All Scripture is God-breathed and is useful for teaching, rebuking, correcting and training in righteousness, so that the servant of God may be thoroughly equipped for every good work.

Paul tells us that Scripture finds its origin in God, who inspired and "breathed into" it. God speaks to us through the human authors who wrote the Bible for the purpose of equipping us in the good work that God wants us to do. God equips us by teaching us, rebuking us, correcting us, and training us. Again, this is work! It's not passively sitting in a lecture. It involves listening to what God is saying and thinking about who God is and what he is doing in the world. It requires that we personally apply what we know about God, what he requires of us, and examine our own hearts to see where we need to grow.

In Isaiah 66:2 God says: "This is the one to whom I will look; he who is humble and contrite in spirit and trembles at my word." I meet very few people who tremble at His word.

—FRANCIS CHAN

Consequently, we must be very careful to teach those we are discipling to follow the teachings of the Bible. Paul goes on to warn us about the importance of knowing and adhering to the Bible's teachings. It's serious!

> In the presence of God and of Christ Jesus, who will judge the living and the dead, and in view of his appearing and his kingdom, I give you this charge: Preach the word; be prepared in season and out of season; correct, rebuke and encourage—with great patience and careful instruction. For the time will come when people will not put up with sound doctrine. Instead, to suit their own desires, they will gather around them a great number of teachers to say what their itching ears want to hear. They will turn their ears away from the truth and turn aside to myths (2 Tim. 4:1–4).

The Word of God is our ultimate and final authority—when we feel like it, and when we don't; when it suits us, and when it doesn't; when we are ready for it, and when we are not. In a recent discipleship.org forum gathering, Francis Chan said this:

Discipleship in this day is a lot of people getting together and sharing their feelings and thoughts. So as leaders we have to teach people to be able to teach others that "your thoughts really don't matter that much, and you can't believe everything you think and feel." And we come under the authority of Scripture. We have to be honest and say, "Look, there's things in this book that I don't agree with, I don't think, I don't feel, but I surrender to it, and when I disagree with this book, I assume God is right and I am wrong." We have to teach them that and show them that. And the greatest thing that any of the guys who discipled me taught me was how to read this book for myself.

Teaching this requires great patience and careful instruction. But if we don't instill this value in the people we're discipling, they will fall for the speculation and the skeptical objections against the Christian faith. We provide the following guidelines to help you lead people along the discipleship journey and to help them study and apply the Bible in their lives. While books, tools, and resources are helpful, never forget that the goal is to get people into Scripture. Too often, disciple making focuses on secondary books or teaching *about* the Bible without a proper focus on the explicit teachings of Scripture.

1. USE THE BIBLE WHEN DISCIPLING NON-CHRISTIANS

Who is the Bible written for? Is it intended for only Christians, something that believers study but not unbelievers? We're not sure where this idea comes from, but some people have the mistaken idea that before you can understand anything in the Bible, you have to be a Christian. Yes, there are passages like 1 Corinthians 1:18 ("The message of the cross is foolishness to those who are perishing") and 2 Corinthians 4:4 ("The god of this age has blinded the minds of unbelievers, so that they cannot see the light of the gospel that displays the glory of Christ"). But these passages speak about sin's power in blinding people from seeing the glory of Jesus and responding to the good news of the gospel.

Does this mean that the Word is useless in leading unbelievers to know God? Of course not! We trust the presence of the Holy Spirit in the process to guide nonbelievers and open their eyes so they can grasp the gospel in a way that will lead them to follow Christ. The Spirit of God uses the Word of God to open hearts and minds to the truth. And one of the best places for someone to begin a search to know God is with a group of three to five other people studying the Bible.[2] Personal Bible study is essential to growth, whether you are an unbeliever, a new believer, or a mature disciple.

Life has a way of changing how we read the Bible and how we experience its supernatural power. Soon after I (Josh) was diagnosed with cancer, I turned to the Bible for comfort and strength. My desperation for God and my hunger for his presence dramatically altered the way I approached his revealed Word. Instead of trying to learn more *about* God, I opened the Bible to encounter God himself. Reading Scripture didn't feel like drudgery or work. It was a lifeline. It was like plugging my heart into the greatest power source in the world. My heart soared as I read, and the promises of God landed firmly in my soul. When my mind wandered or fear crept in, the Spirit brought me back to reality by reminding me of the truth. Cancer opened my eyes to the treasures in the Bible.

We want to model and show people how to engage the Bible with this type of expectancy. The biblical authors captured moments in history when God spoke and acted in decisive ways, and if we want to discern God's will today, we need to know and understand how he spoke in the past. Our study of the Word prepares us to be expectant and to hear God speak as he has spoken in the past.

> As the people of God, we believe the Word of God can be trusted in every way to speak what is true, command what is right, and provide us with what is good.
>
> **—KEVIN DEYOUNG**

In Romans 10:14–17, the apostle Paul points out that until we hear and understand the teachings about Jesus Christ, it is impossible to believe in him. It makes sense, right? How can you trust someone if you don't know anything about them? The primary way people in the first century heard about Jesus was when someone came and told them about Jesus. The message was primarily shared verbally because without printing presses, books were quite rare. As people were exposed to these teachings, they believed them and were saved. Paul writes about how this happens:

How, then, can they call on the one they have not believed in? And how can they believe in the one of whom they have not heard? And how can they hear without someone preaching to them? . . . Consequently, faith comes from hearing the message, and the message is heard through the word of Christ (Rom. 10:14, 17).

Paul's point is simple. People believe because they hear, and they hear because someone preaches the good news to them, so it is essential to have people who know the good news and know how to communicate it to others. Without that, the Word cannot be heard and received. Central to all faith development is exposure to the word of Christ. And that same principle is at work today. For the spiritually curious to become disciples of Jesus, they must be exposed to and understand the clear teachings about Jesus in the Bible.

The Romans 10:17 principle is speaking primarily about non-Christians, but it also applies to people who are already believers. The famous nineteenth-century Christian leader D. L. Moody described his spiritual growth:

I prayed for faith, and thought that someday faith would come down and strike me like lightning. But faith did not seem to come. One day I read in the tenth chapter of Romans . . . I had up to this time closed my Bible and prayed for faith. I now opened my Bible and began to study, and faith has been growing ever since.[3]

> We're going to learn how to do this together, . . . because there's a whole lot of people that need to see what it looks like to follow Jesus in everyday life.
>
> **—JEFF VANDERSTELT**

For Moody, the Bible was instrumental in helping him to experience God. Active exposure to the teachings of the Bible, especially those about Jesus Christ, enabled him to grow spiritually. Hebrews 4:12 teaches this same principle. Although the primary reference in this verse is to the spoken Word of God, the principle applies to the written Word of God as well: "For the word of God is alive and active. Sharper than any double-edged sword, it penetrates even to dividing soul and spirit, joints and marrow; it judges the thoughts and attitudes of the heart." We find this again in Isaiah 55:11, which says of God's Word, given to people: "It will not return to me empty, but will accomplish what I desire and achieve the purpose for which I sent it."

Here is what we've learned so far about the Bible and how God uses the Bible in discipleship:

- God speaks most clearly and directly to people through the Bible.
- We should consistently point people to God's revealed will instead of to our own opinions.
- People cannot be born again or trust and follow Jesus without the Bible.
- We must be able to unveil the true nature of Jesus with the Scriptures.
- The Word of God is indescribably powerful and precious.

2. LOOK FOR JESUS IN ALL PARTS OF THE BIBLE

There's another old expression that we often repeat: "Major on the majors; minor on the minors." Nowhere is this principle more important than when you guide others in a Bible study. There are many things taught in the Bible, but not all of them are central or primary. Jesus is central. The person and teachings of Jesus guide us in how we understand or filter those teachings that are not central and primary. The religious establishment of Jesus' day missed this principle. In Matthew 23:24, Jesus described these leaders as blind guides who would strain out a gnat (focus on a small, incidental teaching) but swallow a camel (miss a major teaching).

> The Bible is the inevitable outcome of God's continuous speech. It is the infallible declaration of His mind.
>
> —A. W. TOZER

The Bible teaches us that certain doctrines are fundamental and central. The central message of the Bible is that we are saved by grace through faith in Jesus Christ. Jesus is the focus, for the gospel is all about him—his life, his teaching, his cross, his resurrection, and his ascending to the place of highest honor in heaven, as he now is our reigning Lord (Acts 10:38–43; 1 Cor. 15:1–8). As we emphasize Jesus' lordship, we want to stress that obedience to Jesus and all that he is and has done for us is the natural response of a heart that has been saved by grace. We respond in gratitude to God's precious gift. Even the Holy Spirit's empowerment within us is a gift, freeing us to respond in faith and faithfulness.

Again, we want to note that simply knowing about Jesus isn't enough to save us. We need understanding and a heart of faith that turns from sin to trust in Christ. We need a heart that is open to correction and responsive to the Lord. This means that the Bible will often say things that we don't want to hear. Mark Twain once said, "Most people are bothered by those passages of Scripture which they cannot understand; but as for me, I have always noticed that the passages of Scripture which trouble me most are those *which I do understand*."[4]

> I just know that a mature person in Christ makes the Bible central to their life. That's how you get mature, and that's how you continue to thrive and abide in Christ in relationship with him. Apart from him, you can do nothing, and God's Word is central to that.
>
> —JIM PUTMAN

In other words, the real problem is not our intellectual grasp of the Bible. It's the heartfelt understanding that leads to conviction and action. We may understand, but if our understanding fails to lead to obedience, we've not truly grasped it with approval and joy. For example, it's not natural to love your enemies and forgive those who have hurt you. But once we grasp Jesus at the center—and our hearts see who he is and what he has done for us—it transforms our study of the Bible. Jesus helps us see what is most important, what is central,

and this mind-set becomes formative in how we study and apply Scripture.

===== PAUSE AND PONDER =====

Why is it helpful to delineate between core doctrines and less important and more personal beliefs?

The Bible is all about Jesus, and every page whispers his name, as a popular story Bible reminds us. Keep the following in mind as you read the Bible with a focus on Jesus:

- Jesus is the main character of the Bible.
- Much of the Bible is simple, but never simplistic.
- Not every doctrine in the Bible is equal in terms of importance.
- If we read the Bible and sincerely look for Jesus, we will find him there.
- The Holy Spirit infuses our engagement with the Bible.

3. TEACH PEOPLE TO READ THE BIBLE THEMSELVES

The only legitimate way to develop an authentic faith grounded in what God says is to study the Bible for ourselves. We love the example of the people of Berea described in the book of Acts. The Bereans were compared to the Thessalonians and, unlike the Thessalonians, they carefully looked into the Scriptures to see what was true so they could know the way of God and properly follow him. In Scripture, the Bereans are highly commended for seeking to know the truth of Scripture and searching out the true meaning.

> Now the Berean Jews were of more noble character than those in Thessalonica, for they received the message with great eagerness and examined the Scriptures every day to see if what Paul said was true (Acts 17:11).

Like the Bereans, if we truly want to be noble in God's sight, we must examine the Scriptures in all things to determine the truth for ourselves. As disciple makers, we need to teach this principle to our disciples. *Yes,* we may sometimes need teachers and aids to help us. *Yes,* there are parts of the Bible that are complex and difficult to understand. And *yes,* different well-studied and highly educated Christians understand some things in different ways. But there is also a remarkable agreement among Christians on the Great

Tradition—the core teachings that reflect what Christians at all times in all places have generally believed.

Remember, we do not follow people; we follow Jesus, and we learn how to follow him through the teachings of the Bible. As a disciple, I am responsible for the way I live my faith and the choices I make. And we teach our disciples the same. We teach people to depend on God, not on us.

There are some things that we will not know for ourselves until we seek out God's teaching in Scripture *by ourselves!* This is a fundamental principle of the Christian life:

> And without faith it is impossible to please God, because anyone who comes to him must believe that he exists and that he rewards those who earnestly seek him (Heb. 11:6).

> "You will seek me and find me when you seek me with all your heart. I will be found by you," declares the Lord (Jer. 29:13–14).

The best way to come to know God and know the teachings of the Bible is by directly studying Scripture, not just the thoughts, traditions, and teachings of men.[5]

Of course, we can do both, but we want to make sure that we are prioritizing our study of the Bible, not replacing it with other books and teachings.

> No one succeeds at the highest level in sports without working out. No one makes it in music without lots of practice. No one excels in scholarship without years of study. And no one makes it far in the school of holiness without hours and days and years in the Word.
>
> **—KEVIN DEYOUNG**

Teaching people to read the Bible for themselves means that:

- There is no substitute for the discipline of personal Bible reading.
- For our faith in Jesus to be authentic, we must look for him with all our hearts in the Scriptures.
- Our thoughts and conclusions about the Bible should come mainly from what we've discovered ourselves, not on what other people have told us.
- As disciple makers, we should equip the people we're investing in to read the Bible for themselves.

4. APPROACH THE BIBLE WITH A HUMBLE HEART FOCUSED ON OBEDIENCE

In the Great Commission of Matthew 28:19–20, Jesus told us that we make disciples by teaching them to obey everything that Jesus commanded. Think about that for a moment. Everything Jesus commanded. That's a big deal! To really do this, we will need a lot of help. We're going to need other people and strategic processes that challenge us, hold us accountable, and give us examples of how to live in obedience as disciples.

PAUSE AND PONDER

Do you think it's possible to truly obey all of Jesus' teachings, as he commanded?

The root of all obedience that honors God—the nonnegotiable starting point for understanding and applying the Bible—is a tender heart for the author of Scripture. God speaks to his people through his Word, calling us to change and obey. The Christian leader Martin Luther described his own experience:

The Bible is alive, it speaks to me. It has feet, it runs after me. It has hands, it lays hold of me.[6]

Of course, we can resist and ignore what God is saying. The Bible speaks of having a hard heart, a heart that is unresponsive to God's Word. The power of the Bible is effective and life-transforming, depending on a person's spiritual disposition before God. We must teach those we disciple that our spiritual disposition before God is fundamental. In other words, there is a right way and a wrong way to engage the Bible. A tender, responsive, obedient spirit that is eager to honor the Lord will lead to deep and dramatic transformation. When God shows us something in his Word, it's not just something to be analyzed, negotiated, or—worse—ignored. It's meant to be treasured and applied. Disobedience to God's Word leaves us unchanged and feeds our self-deception so we wander around in blindness.

Teach those you disciple *how* to approach the Bible. Model for them what it means to prayerfully ask God to speak to you. Show them how to ask questions without being suspicious or doubting, but truly wrestling with God in faith.

- There are many misguided approaches to Bible reading.

- The best way to engage the Bible is with a tender and humble heart.
- It's safer and easier to study or analyze the contents of the Bible than to obey the God who is revealed in the Bible.
- We should not only read the Bible; we should allow it to read us.
- People are deeply transformed from the inside out when they obey the Bible's teachings.

> It's not just passing on the information, but the example of a man or woman of God who trembles at his word and says, "Look, that's what the Word says, so I did that this week."
>
> —FRANCIS CHAN

WHAT DOES IT LOOK LIKE TO USE THE BIBLE IN DISCIPLESHIP?

There are many ways to use the Bible in the discipleship process, more than we can possibly cover in this chapter. Our goal has been to give you a sense of the nonnegotiable importance of relying on and using the Bible as you disciple. Remember, the first thing you will want to do before you focus on teaching others is to spend time seeking to encounter God in the Bible for yourself. Plan the what, when, and how of your own personal Bible reading and make it a nonnegotiable part of your life. Out of this habitual experience, you will naturally have things to share with others.

Second, we suggest that you work with other leaders in your church to find some good material to help you study the Bible. For example, in our home church, we have different levels of material that we recommend for different spiritual seekers. At a basic level, we have a small booklet that explains how to become a disciple of Jesus. At the next level, we have about eight simple Bible studies that get people into the Bible (under the key topics). And for serious adults, we have our "Foundation Studies: The Storyline of the Real Jesus."[7]

Finally, we want to emphasize that as wonderful as it is to have regular daily time in the Word, we also need to read and study together.[8] As our friend Jim Putman says, "You can know the Word and not be mature. But you cannot be mature without knowing the Word. Study the Bible with others who are seeking spiritual growth. Ask real-life questions, talk it out, and most importantly, challenge each other to apply what you're reading."

- It is impossible to make disciples of Jesus without the Bible.
- It is critical to find ways to let the Bible speak for itself and allow people to explore in a safe environment.
- Time in the Bible should mean a stronger faith, obedience, a focus on Jesus, and the upholding of God's ways.
- As disciple makers, we need Bible study plans that we use to guide others.
- The purpose of the Bible is to unveil the character of God as revealed in the person of Jesus and to equip us to flourish as God's children.

FOR REFLECTION AND CONVERSATION

1. Why is "how we live, not what we know" the primary focus of discipleship?

2. What does it mean to say that studying the Word of God creates faith? Explain how this happens.

3. In what way is Jesus central to personally knowing the Bible?

4. Who were the Bereans, and what is so valuable about the way they approached the Bible?

Chapter 8

SPIRIT

"I will ask the Father, and he will give you
another advocate to help you and be with
you forever—the Spirit of truth."

JOHN 14:16-17

The Holy Spirit is sometimes called the neglected person of the Trinity. In many churches, you won't hear much talk about the Spirit, and if you do, it will typically focus on the gifts or the fruit of the Spirit. But the Bible tells us that the work of the Spirit is not just something we add onto the Christian life. Without the Spirit, the Christian life is impossible. Unless the Holy Spirit is present and doing his work, nobody can be born again or grow in Christlikeness. Without the work of the Holy Spirit, we cannot make disciples of Jesus.

In this chapter, we cannot cover everything the Holy Spirit does in the Christian life and in the world. Instead, we will focus on the work of the Spirit in the disciple-making process. To begin, we'd like you to imagine that you and a few of your closest friends are on an extended road trip across the United States. The goal of your grand vacation is to see the most beautiful and breathtaking landscapes all across the country. To make the most of this once-in-a-lifetime experience, you have spent months planning and preparing. You've done everything you can to ensure that this trip will be unforgettable. As the departure date nears, you can hardly wait to hit the road!

You've talked about this trip so many times with your family and coworkers that they've grown sick of hearing about it. You can barely sleep the night before you leave, and then the day of the trip finally arrives. Your bags are packed. All the research has been done. You and your friends load your luggage. You make sure the navigation system is ready. Everyone gets in the car. It's finally time to go. But there's a problem. A *big* problem.

There is no fuel in the car. How in the world did this happen?

You have a well-thought-out plan, but the engine won't start. Your strategy is solid, but the car isn't going anywhere. You have all the information you need, but you're stuck.

Okay, so this scenario is a little silly. After all, who would do all of that planning and then forget to fill the gas tank. But as crazy as this sounds, it's uncomfortably similar to how many people approach discipleship. We commonly see people trying in their own strength and through their own willpower and effort to make spiritual progress without the power of the Holy Spirit. But this process isn't natural or easy. Every step we make is opposed by our sinful nature, by the fallen world we live in, and by our enemy,

Satan. Attempting to do anything resembling spiritual growth without the supernatural assistance of the Holy Spirit is like embarking on a cross-country road trip in a vehicle that has no fuel. This has one direct implication for us: it is impossible to embrace Jesus' method of discipleship without purposefully living under the influence of the Spirit.

> The Spirit is not a passive power that we can wield as we choose. The Spirit is God, a Being who requires that we submit ourselves to be led by Him.
>
> —FRANCIS CHAN

The Spirit is the agent that draws us to follow Jesus (John 16:7–11; 1 John 2:20–27); that changes us into Jesus' image (2 Cor. 3:17–18; Gal. 5:22–23); and that powers our partnership in Jesus' mission (Matt. 28:20; Acts 1:6–8). The Great Commission ends with a promise. Jesus tells us that he will be present with us through his Holy Spirit as we make disciples: "And surely I am with you always, to the very end of the age" (Matt. 28:20). We depend on this promise. The Spirit's presence needs to undergird all that we do as disciple makers.

We can't emphasize this enough. I (Bobby) gathered a group of national leaders for a discussion and planning session for one of our national disciple-making forums (see www.discipleship.org). I was very excited to talk with leaders that I respected, and after our initial discussion I was feeling good about how we had all come together to agree on the various elements of discipleship reflected in Jesus' method and model. Until Francis Chan confronted me.

"Why are we not placing more emphasis on the Holy Spirit?" he said. "Uh, well . . . I guess we just assumed it," I said. "Well, let's not do that," he said. Immediately, I knew that he was right. We had been assuming the Spirit, and in assuming the work of the Spirit, we were neglecting his essential role. The things that you assume, like the work of the Holy Spirit, can easily be forgotten. Over time, as our discussion broadened to include diverse voices from the global church, we've begun to emphasize the role of the Holy Spirit more explicitly.

Our definition of a *disciple* is based on Matthew 4:19, a watershed passage on discipleship, where Jesus said: "Follow me, and I will make you fishers of men" (ESV). As Jim Putman puts it, "In the definition is the invitation." A genuine disciple of Jesus is marked by three characteristics—a disciple *follows Jesus*, is *changed by Jesus*, and is *committed to the mission of Jesus*. The work of the Spirit includes all three, but in this chapter we will spend most of our time focused on the middle part—being changed by Jesus. Jesus does this work of transformation through the Holy Spirit. But how does the Holy Spirit change people? How can we as disciple makers rely on the Spirit to guide our disciple-making efforts?

> The Christian's life in all its aspects—intellectual and ethical, devotional and relational, upsurging in worship and outgoing in witness—is supernatural; only the Spirit can initiate and sustain it.
>
> —J. I. PACKER

1. HELP PEOPLE TO SEE THE SPIRIT AT WORK IN REPENTANCE.

We cannot turn away from our sin and toward Jesus unless we are first aware of our own sinfulness. We cannot sense regret and sorrow for our acts of foolishness and rebellion unless we are conscious that they are displeasing to God. We cannot be saved unless we first realize we are sinners.

How do we develop this awareness of sin? There may be many factors that lead us to an awareness of sin. For some, they begin to reap what they have sown, or suffer the consequences of sinful choices. Perhaps their reckless living results in an awful tragedy. This may come in the form of a financial collapse following dishonest business practices, a deadly illness sparked by unhealthy habits or careless living, or a legal trial triggered by law breaking. The Bible is clear that God has instituted a moral order to the world, and in many situations we reap the fruit of what we have sown in this life. For some, tasting those consequences prepares the heart to hear and respond to the good news of the gospel of Jesus.

> The fruit of the Spirit gives a sure sign of transformed character. When our deepest attitudes and dispositions are those of Jesus, it is because we have learned to let the Spirit foster his life in us.
>
> —DALLAS WILLARD

Others will say that they were awakened to their personal sinfulness through someone who taught them basic biblical truths about sin. The apostle Paul tells us that God gave us his law as a teacher to prepare our hearts for Christ and the message of the gospel (Gal. 3:24). The law of God teaches us to recognize sin (Rom. 7:7). Learning about the holiness of God and how

we fall short of his perfect goodness can also prepare a heart to hear the good news of the gospel. When we understand that we are lost without the grace of God, we begin to recognize our need for a Savior.

Jesus clearly taught that however we come to recognize our sin, conviction is always the Spirit's work: "When he comes, he will prove the world to be in the wrong about sin and righteousness and judgment" (John 16:8). Knowing that conviction is the Spirit's task takes a burden off our shoulders as we proclaim the gospel. We do not need to prove to others that they are sinners in need of redemption. We do not need to focus our attention on how bad they are. The Spirit will use God's Word to do that work as we lead people through what the Bible teaches.

The Holy Spirit's priority is to point us to Jesus and to lead his followers into all truth. On the night before his crucifixion, Jesus said this to his disciples, "The Advocate, the Holy Spirit, whom the Father will send in my name, will teach you all things and will remind you of everything I have said to you" (John 14:26). The Holy Spirit came to enable us to know Jesus through the miracle of the new birth and to give us the power to live an abundant life which Jesus promised to all who trust and follow him.

On one occasion Jesus told a devoutly

religious man named Nicodemus that he had to be born again in order to see and enter the kingdom of heaven—he had to start all over again (John 3:1–15). The basis of this rebirth is the work of God's Spirit. Jesus said the Spirit would work in a person's life like the wind. We cannot see the wind itself when it is blowing, but we can note the effects:

> The wind blows wherever it pleases. You hear its sound, but you cannot tell where it comes from or where it is going. So it is with everyone born of the Spirit (John 3:8).

In this way Jesus gave us a guide for how the Holy Spirit works in the disciple. The Spirit will be known more by its influence in our lives than by a direct and tangible experience.

PAUSE AND PONDER

What did you grow up hearing about the Holy Spirit? How has your understanding of him changed over time?

The Holy Spirit catalyzes conversion by leading people to repent and believe in Jesus. At the heart of Jesus' message was a call to respond to his proclamation of God's reign:

"The kingdom of God has come near. Repent and believe the good news!" (Mark 1:15). To understand conversion, we must look more closely at how we personally respond to the gospel, how we respond to Jesus' invitation to repent and believe the good news.

> The Holy Spirit illuminates the minds of people, makes us yearn for God, and takes spiritual truth and makes it understandable to us.
>
> —BILLY GRAHAM

Repentance is a radical turning within the human heart (Luke 1:16–17; 2 Cor. 3:16–17). This turning involves our entire being. It begins with an *intellectual* change, a metamorphosis of the mind, an altered opinion about ourselves, about how we have been living, and about what we have done. What we once thought was okay, we now view as sin. We used to think of ourselves as basically good people, but we now know that we are "poor in spirit" (Matt. 5:3) and desperately need God.

Repentance also includes an *emotional* change. Like Paul, we now hate what we find ourselves doing (Rom. 7:15). Repentance involves a transformation of the *will*. A changed opinion and heartfelt, sorrowful regret naturally lead us to desire to alter who we are and what we do. No longer do we want to live as we did in the past. Instead, we resolve to go in a different direction.

Think of an area of your life that you once felt okay about, but now even the thought of it brings you shame.

Let's say it was the way you sought entertainment. Perhaps you used to watch movies or TV shows that promoted or celebrated sins that are clearly condemned in the Bible. You didn't think much of it in your former life, but your relationship with Jesus has forever altered your perspective. The thought of celebrating a sinful behavior is unacceptable to you.

Maybe it was the way you responded to pain. When the pressures of life mounted, you turned to created things that are inherently good—like food, your career, relationships, or sex—to bring peace amidst the chaos. But you've learned that when you turn a good thing into an ultimate thing, you end up empty and frustrated and not like Jesus. You may have even depended on destructive things when you were stressed out—like alcohol, drugs, or pornography—to numb the pain inside. Now you know that false gods always overpromise and under deliver. Jesus has set you free from their tyranny, and now you're committed to living in the light.

That is repentance. Unless we recognize our great need for redemption, we will not cry out to God to save us. By itself, however, repentance is not enough. Truth be told, we cannot fully make amends for the past. And we aren't strong or righteous enough to break the bondage of sin. Despite our reflection, regret, and resolve, sin continues to hold us captive. A person who is caught in an insidious addiction to pornography cannot break free from such an entanglement with remorse alone. The compulsive worrier cannot simply stop worrying by feeling convicted about the sinfulness of worry. In addition to turning *from* sin, we must turn *to* Jesus.

In order for repentance to finish its work, *faith* must be added to the equation. Our faith isn't generic. The object of our faith is Jesus. The Spirit enables us to see Jesus as our wonderful Savior from sin who has conquered death and is returning soon to establish his forever kingdom. We have faith in who Jesus is (Lord, example, and teacher) and what Jesus has done for us—as the atoning sacrifice for our sin who clothes us in his righteousness, enabling us to stand before God. And we have faith in Jesus' guidance, what Jesus does in us, and what Jesus will do for us, placing our hope in his future promises.

- People become conscious of their sin by the Spirit's work.
- We do not see the Spirit directly; we see the Spirit's effect (like the wind).

- The Spirit works within us to change our hearts, minds, and wills in regard to sin.
- The Spirit works as we see the negative reality of sin in our lives.
- We turn away from sin and to Jesus, the answer to our sin.

---

2. HELP PEOPLE SEE THE SPIRIT *ENABLING* THEIR RESPONSE.

It is often shocking and even horrifying to become aware of our sinfulness. Deep sorrow may drag us down. We may fall into hopelessness and despair. However, the Spirit's goal is *conviction*, not destruction. He desires that we not only see our sin but also turn to God for forgiveness and healing. Thus, in addition to convicting us of sin, the Spirit issues a call to sinners to receive the saving grace of God.

In Matthew 22, Jesus told a story about a wedding party hosted by a king. The king's servants announce his invitation throughout the entire land. Through the words of his servants, the king himself calls the guests to attend and enjoy the banquet. As human messengers announce the good news, the Spirit calls the hearers to respond.

This means that the Spirit animates human words in mysterious ways. As we communicate the gospel, at some point our words become the very words of God. Through Isaiah, for example, God compared the power of his word with the life-giving force of water:

> "As the rain and the snow come down from heaven, and do not return to it without watering the earth and making it bud and flourish, so that it yields seed for the sower and bread for the eater, so is my word that goes out from my mouth: It will not return to me empty, but will accomplish what I desire and achieve the purpose for which I sent it" (Isa. 55:10–11).

That is why the Bible encourages us to know and share God's Word: "How beautiful on the mountains are the feet of those who bring good news" (Isa. 52:7; Rom. 10:15). The voice of the messenger is the voice of God. As Paul said concerning himself and his associates: "We are therefore Christ's ambassadors, as though God were making his appeal through us. We implore you on Christ's behalf: Be reconciled to God" (2 Cor. 5:20).

How can someone receive the gospel in faith when they cannot understand it? For the unbeliever, the message of Jesus is incomprehensible and inconceivable. The apostle Paul attributes this inability to rightly understand the Word to Satan.

The god of this age has blinded the minds of unbelievers, so that they cannot see the light of the gospel that displays the glory of Christ, who is the image of God (2 Cor. 4:4).

People cannot see, understand, or receive the gospel without the Holy Spirit. The enemy has blinded them, and the veil will not be removed unless the Spirit moves. Spiritual blindness is an irreversible condition apart from the Spirit. The Spirit opens our minds so that we can perceive the truth of the gospel. "For God, who said, 'Let light shine out of darkness,' made his light shine in our hearts to give us the light of the knowledge of God's glory displayed in the face of Christ" (2 Cor. 4:6).

The Spirit is the ultimate change agent. By convicting us of sin and enabling us to repent and place faith in Jesus, he initiates the salvation process. We pray that people will not resist him (Acts 7:51). Those who repent, surrender, and place their faith in him receive the Spirit's indwelling presence (Acts 2:38; Eph. 1:13–14). He then guides us in a lifelong *process*, not a one-time event. It's a journey that begins with conversion, continues throughout life, and comes to completion at Jesus' return. Just as physical birth is not the *goal* but only the beginning of physical life, so also the new birth—conversion—is only the beginning of our eternal life.

> Being the church that Jesus intended means that we must participate in God's eternal purposes for his world. Renewal means more than reinventing ourselves; it means rediscovering the primal power of the Spirit and the gospel already present in the life of the church.
>
> —ALAN HIRSCH

This means that our attempts at outreach are not merely directed toward winning the lost. Our responsibility is not finished when they are baptized and join a local church. Rather, our goal is *disciple making*. This must also mean that we should not view our own salvation solely in terms of the moment of conversion. Instead, salvation is an all-encompassing, supernatural Spirit-directed process. Conversion is the starting line. It is the point where God comes to indwell us and lead us into the image of his Son.

- Satan has blinded the minds of unbelievers, and the Spirit opens their eyes.

- The Spirit of God makes the words of God powerful and effective in our hearts.
- The Spirit is the light of Christ, illuminating the things of God within us.
- The Spirit takes up residence at our conversion and invisibly guides and leads us.

---

3. HELP PEOPLE WITH SPIRITUAL PRACTICES AND SUFFERING.

Most Christians want to grow, and they need the Spirit's help. The process is called *sanctification* by theologians. Sanctification is simply the ongoing process whereby the Holy Spirit transforms us into the image of Jesus. This metamorphosis comes in at least two ways. Neither is easy; both are difficult. Neither is instantaneous; both are processes.

There is a *disciplined, habitual* approach to sanctification. These are the historic practices of prayer, Scripture reading, fasting, service, and confession. By practicing these disciplines, we open ourselves up to the Holy Spirit's transformative power. Nobody floats into spiritual maturity by accident. They get there on purpose. Paul said that people are trained to be godly (1 Tim. 4:7). Any disciple who ignores these spiritual practices puts their spiritual life

in danger and will find themselves fearful and empty inside. The Spirit is willing and able to change our hearts, but we must do our part. Spiritual practices (prayer, Scripture, etc.) shape our inner life as intentional daily habits. We must set aside time and orient our lives through these practices. It takes effort and consistency. The long-term result is dramatic character transformation.

There is also the path of suffering. At some point, it happens to everybody. The realities of living in a broken, corrupt world will pounce on us without warning. They come from out of nowhere. We don't see them coming. They happen to us. Our daily habits may prepare us for them—that is the value of spiritual training, but we have no control over the trials that come our way.

These fires burn through our lives in many different ways. Physical suffering—whether cancer, chronic illness, or genetic disabilities—is one fire. Emotional suffering—childhood trauma, mental illness, losses of various kinds—is another kind of fire. Then there are the relational difficulties that pierce our hearts. When we are betrayed, insulted, gossiped about—when we are sinned against—this is something that happens *to us*. We did not ask for it. In fact, we perhaps never imagined it. It is a trial, a test. It is a burning fire that will either destroy us or refine us. It is a moment when we will reject God's heart of forgiveness for others, or we will embrace his mercy for ourselves as well as for others. It is an occasion for spiritual transformation.

> Would you say that your life is marked right now by desperation for the Spirit of God?
>
> —DAVID PLATT

We don't get to choose our struggles, but God has given us the freedom to choose how we respond to them. "Life happens," as they say. It can be very ugly, horrid, evil stuff, or it can be seemingly minor frustrations and unmet expectations. Both, however, are opportunities for spiritual growth. When "life" happens, God is present in ways that transcend our ability to grasp. He is also present to lovingly refine and/or purge us. It becomes part of the process of transformation, just as Jesus himself was formed spiritually through his suffering. (He was made perfect by the things he suffered—Heb. 5:8–9.)

Dallas Willard defined pain as a time "when we bump into reality." But the hurt, by God's grace and power, is a way forward into the Father's heart, participation in the Son's suffering, and communion with the groaning

Spirit. Paul the apostle taught about the purpose of pain in Romans 5:3–5:

> We know that suffering produces perseverance; perseverance, character; and character, hope. And hope does not put us to shame, because God's love has been poured out into our hearts through the Holy Spirit, who has been given to us.

God uses suffering to build our perseverance, shape our character, and increase our hope. Perseverance in the Bible means steadfast adherence to a course of action in spite of difficulties and testing. As we go through trials, we develop greater perseverance (or endurance) to deal with life's challenges. As the Spirit helps us to deal with more hardship, he brings out character (or resilience). In essence, character exposes the quality of what's being tested. Pain unmasks our true nature.

When I (Josh) bumped into the reality of my mortality when I was diagnosed with cancer, I had some choices to make. Will I surrender to the purifying power of pain and be transformed, or will I fight against it and drown in a sea of despair? Will I let God expose my arrogance in assuming that I will live a long life? Will I trust the incredible wisdom that God revealed to Paul in Romans 5 about the purpose of suffering, or will I lean on my own wisdom? Everyone will face these choices—probably several times when it's all said and done.

In the heat of suffering, God gives grace for us to endure. A goldsmith uses heat under a smelting pot to bring the impurities to the top so they can be skimmed off, leaving only the pure gold. In the same way, God uses pain to bring out the impurities in our lives so they can be removed. Character that is sanctified by the Spirit becomes progressively more stable and is therefore able to focus more attentively on the things of God.

But the process doesn't end with solid character. The Spirit unleashes *hope* in suffering. Hope is the confident, joyful expectation of what the Lord has promised. As disciples of Jesus, we must embrace the hope of the empty tomb and remember that nothing is impossible with God. The same power that raised Jesus from the dead resides in us (Rom. 8:11; Eph. 1:19–20)!

We experience the transforming power of the Holy Spirit through intentional spiritual practices like prayer, reading Scripture, and fasting. These habits train us to attend to the presence of God, discern the will of God, and display the character of God. We are also shaped by suffering. The Spirit uses pain to dethrone our idols, show us our true selves, and teach us how to trust Jesus. As Paul told the church in Corinth, "And we all, who with unveiled faces contemplate the Lord's glory, *are being transformed into his image with ever-increasing glory*, which comes from the Lord, who is the Spirit" (2 Cor. 3:18, emphasis added).

We should follow Jesus who practiced Scripture memory, fasting, and solitude.

- As the apostle Paul taught, we should train ourselves to be godly.
- Christians wrongly, but naturally, think we will avoid suffering.
- Sufferings have the unique ability to shape us into more godly people.
- The Spirit will use our sufferings to develop godly hope.

4. GIVE PEOPLE ENCOURAGEMENT ABOUT GOD'S HELP.

Many people are frightened when they think about committing themselves to trust and follow Jesus. When they truly grasp what Jesus calls for in their lives, they think they cannot do it. They look at seemingly devout disciples as highly moral people who set an unattainable standard. "I respect them for how they live," they say, "but I can't see myself doing that."

I (Bobby) had a friend who held back from committing his life to Jesus for many years. He was a highly respected medical scientist, so I assumed that his barrier to faith was intellectual. He kept telling me that he was not ready. Then one day I figured out what was holding him back. He is a very sincere person with high moral standards, and suddenly I saw it. He knew that he could never live up to the high calling that Jesus was calling him to live. He didn't want to fail, so he held back from committing.

This problem is common, and it is often stated as a question: "Do I have the strength and ability to be a disciple of Jesus?" I'm glad that people are asking this question, because it tells me that they are taking the call to follow Jesus seriously. My answer to this question is always the same: "No . . . you do not have the strength and ability. You don't have what it takes." You do not have the strength, and you do not have the ability—in yourself—to follow Jesus, be changed by Jesus, and join the kingdom mission of Jesus. But that misses the good news of the gospel! Those who think this way are still harboring the false hope that they can somehow try harder and become a better person. They haven't given in to the truth that they need a Savior. We don't need a hand to help us, we need to be raised from the dead!

The gospel is good news because it tells us that none of us are good enough or strong enough to do what Jesus asks of us. But God promises to give you the strength and ability when you make the decision to trust and follow Jesus. God works through our weakness, our failures and mistakes, and enables us to follow Jesus by the presence and power of his Holy Spirit.

PAUSE AND PONDER

When making disciples, it's helpful to get clear on God's part, their part, and my part. What is our part in the disciple-making process? What is God's part? What is their (the folks we're investing in) part?

The Spirit of God indwells us to help us to follow Jesus, be changed by Jesus, and be committed to the mission of Jesus. As you read through each of the ways that the Holy Spirit helps change people in the discipleship process, we recommend two questions our friend Alex Absalom asks the people he disciples.

His first question draws attention to the presence of the Holy Spirit in the discipleship process (as described below). Alex asks, "What is God showing you?" It is a simple but profound question to begin a discussion about the things the Holy Spirit is revealing. Often, this may be a deeper awareness of who Jesus is or what he has done. It might be a new awareness of who you are in Jesus, your identity as someone loved by God. Knowing what God has done for us will lead to our response, and that's the next question we ask.

His second question is an obedience-based question, for we should be encouraging people to respond to the Spirit: "What are you doing about it?" We commend the use of such questions in personal discipleship. They not only surface the work of the Holy Spirit, they also guide people so that they are listening for the promptings of the Holy Spirit.

HOW DO WE ENCOURAGE THE WORK OF THE SPIRIT?

The first thing we should do to encourage openness to the work of the Spirit is to regularly pray for the Spirit's presence and help. We pray like Paul did that the Spirit would bring wisdom and knowledge to those we are discipling (and to us). Paul expressed it this way in Colossians 1:9–10:

We have not stopped praying for you. We continually ask God to fill you with the knowledge of his will through all the wisdom and understanding that the Spirit gives, so that you may live a life worthy of the Lord and please him in every way.

We often talk about our need for a personal relationship with God, and that is good. But more often the Bible talks about being led by the Spirit, filled with the Spirit, and in step with the Spirit. When we talk about the work of the Spirit, we align with God's Word and gain a better sense of God's presence in making disciples. Let's not forget the Holy Spirit! In the words we use, in our prayers, and in what we study, we make every effort to draw attention to the person and work of the Holy Spirit.

- The Spirit is active and he is God at work, empowering disciple making.
- The Spirit makes our lives attractive and connects us with the right people if we will seek God's guidance.
- The Holy Spirit is able to help you see where a person is with the Lord and empower you to meet them in that place and encourage them appropriately.
- Resist the urge to push or make something happen for someone. You are not the Holy Spirit! Your job is to love and equip. It's the Spirit's job to convict and change.

FOR REFLECTION AND CONVERSATION

1. How do we rely on God to convict lost people? Why does the Spirit not bring people to Jesus apart from the Word?

2. What are the core practices that enable us to open ourselves up to the Spirit's power and guidance?

3. How do we stifle or work against the Spirit?

4. How do you know when you are being led by the Spirit?

5. How do you know if someone else is being led by the Spirit?

6. How does the Spirit produce fruit over time in the life of a disciple?

Chapter 9

JOURNEY

> He is the one we proclaim, admonishing and
> teaching everyone with all wisdom, so that we
> may present everyone fully mature in Christ.
> — COLOSSIANS 1:28

For many Christians today, the word *salvation* implies an event—a prayer, a baptism, a moment. "When were you saved?" someone might ask us, looking for a specific date and time. And while there are times when the Bible speaks of a time of conversion, more often when the New Testament writers speak of salvation, they describe it as a *process* (see 2 Cor. 3:18; Eph. 4:14; Phil. 3:12–14). We are saved at our conversion (justification), and then we work out our conversion through life (sanctification). Salvation includes both aspects. It is an extended narrative of ongoing transformation, whereby the Holy Spirit gradually brings us into conformity with the character of Jesus.

The material that we present in this chapter may be new to some of you, especially those who have been taught that salvation is a one-time event, and there isn't much we do in this life until we head to heaven or Jesus returns. But this understanding of a journey—a process of spiritual growth—is a vitally important perspective in disciple making that we have found to be very helpful.[1] We want to explain the journey of development that leads people to become fully Christlike. From our new birth to spiritual parenthood we find a distinct, though at times disjointed and unpredictable, story of development and growth where the Holy Spirit leads us on a shared, formative journey.

Both of us began to treasure Jesus as adults, and we naively assumed that true Christians *automatically* formed their lives around whatever Jesus taught—that it was effortless. We're not sure where we got that idea. Maybe it came from the Christians we knew at the time, or maybe it was the teaching we received, or the degree to which those around us emphasized "living the Christian life." We aren't sure, but this false assumption is both unrealistic and unbiblical. We freely admit that we were blind to our own pride. We didn't realize that bringing your entire life into alignment with the teachings of Jesus is a lifelong project, filled with growth and failures. It's a journey of growing in grace.

Remember, a disciple is a person who is *following* Jesus, being *changed* by Jesus, and *committed to the mission* of Jesus. By definition, discipleship is a process because I must learn how to trust and follow. Formation is a lifelong journey, and faithfully joining a mission requires understanding and developed effectiveness in it. The key words here are *process, formation, development, story,* and especially, *journey.*

When guiding people along the discipleship journey, we want to consider our interconnectedness as we travel. While the disciple cannot very effectively travel the journey without help, the responsibility for spiritual growth must never rest on the disciple maker alone. Based on Matthew 28:19–20, we teach that there are three parts to the discipleship process: (1) my part as disciple maker, (2) the disciple's part, and (3) God's part. Here's a summary:

God's role: God is the agent of transformation in the disciple-making process. God promises to work by his Spirit to bring forth fruit in the lives of both the disciple and the disciple maker.

The disciple maker's role: The one "making" the disciple must intentionally pursue, encourage, teach, coach, and pray for the person in his or her spiritual journey.

The disciple's role: A disciple must embrace and maintain an attitude of humility and hunger, as God works through the disciple maker, and respond in obedience to the teachings of Jesus.

We can always trust God to be present and powerful, but we also need to remember that disciples have to choose the path of discipleship out of the love God has shown us. I must accurately understand my responsibility as a leader in light of God's role, learning to be patient and resting in God's plan and timing while being alert to opportunities he provides.

> A farmer is helpless to grow grain; all he can do is provide the right conditions for the growing of grain. He cultivates the ground, he plants the seed, he waters the plants, and then the natural forces of the earth take over and up comes the grain. . . . This is the way it is with the Spiritual Disciplines—they are a way of sowing to the Spirit. . . . By themselves the Spiritual Disciplines can do nothing; they can only get us to the place where something can be done.
>
> —RICHARD FOSTER

Ever since I (Josh) began making disciples, I have found myself overestimating my role in the discipleship process. Sometimes I'm tempted to assume responsibility for someone else's spiritual growth. I feel as though I have to make something happen. But as we saw in the last chapter, that is the territory of the Holy Spirit. We cannot make people do certain things, and it's unloving and unhelpful to even try. My job as the disciple maker is to help a person I'm investing in to see a tangible next step. By sharing my life and experiences with someone else, God shines some light on their path so they can take another step toward Jesus.

Discipleship requires us to walk with people through the next step in their journey to be like Jesus. We have already explained how important relationships, Jesus, intentionality, the Bible, and the Spirit are to the discipleship process. Now we want to emphasize the need for the traceable development path the Bible reveals. Disciple makers are conscious of this path and lead those they are discipling accordingly. It is an incremental journey, with next steps for everyone along the path.

Harpeth Christian Church uses the diagram below to offer a visual introduction to the discipleship journey. The discipleship journey begins at the far left with people who are spiritually lost, and then, crossing the canyon, it moves to the far right, with spiritual parents who are disciple makers.

Various places in the New Testament detail the journey depicted in the diagram. Jesus and the apostles modeled what it looks like to guide disciples on a development journey. Sometimes they were on track, but many times they were off track, with bad ideas and willful disobedience. Jesus was patient with his disciples, correcting their misunderstandings, challenging their selfishness,

and loving them when they failed. God's love and grace, fed to disciples through the Word and the Spirit, are the sustenance for the journey.

We want to make a crucial point here. The diagram presents a clear, linear progression of growth. But real life is not this simple. The discipleship journey is unpredictable and painful at times. More often than not, the path looks more like a bunch of zig-zags than a neat, straight line. No two journeys are the same. God has placed everyone on an individualized spiritual growth track, and each story has unique features. Trying to systematize God's work of transformation in a person would be impossible. The diagram is useful because it shows us the process of growth, and we can see general principles at work, but the contours of each person's journey with Jesus are sacred and unique.

The discipleship journey includes five key stages. This material is simply an introduction. We recommend picking up the *Real-Life Discipleship Training Manual* as the best way to understand this material at a deeper level.[2] When disciple makers understand this journey, it helps them to have the right expectations and to guide people appropriately at each stage.

PRE-CONVERSION STAGE: SPIRITUALLY DEAD—THEY DO NOT HAVE THE HOLY SPIRIT

At the far left in the diagram are those described in Ephesians 2:1–5 as "dead in [their] transgressions and sins." People in this stage have not yet accepted Jesus as Lord and Savior. They may completely reject God, they may be seeking God, they may call themselves "spiritual," they may even claim to know God or call themselves Christian, but there is no real, observable fruit in their life. Even though some have claimed they know Jesus, they do not have the Holy Spirit living in them (at least that you can tell).

> To live by grace means to acknowledge my whole life story, the light side and the dark.
>
> —BRENNAN MANNING

My wife and I (Bobby) met with some of our neighbors a few days ago. A couple doors down from us lives a family from India, and my wife regularly reaches out to them, and on one occasion, we had them in our home. We have connected with them because we want to be good neighbors. That's our first priority—to treat them with kindness, respect, and love because we want to. We would do this regardless of whether they believe in Jesus or not. But we also believe that it's no accident that they are our neighbors, and we want to build a relationship with them in the hope that we can share the good news about Jesus with them.

We have been praying for this family, praying that God would use us to lead them to Jesus. So this family has been on my mind and in my heart. I remind myself that they are blind to spiritual things. To my knowledge, they have not heard the gospel or the Word of God. They do not see the world the way I see it. To this family, we are just random neighbors at this point.

People like this need our prayers, but they also need a relationship with a Christian believer where they can hear the Word of God and their hearts can be enlightened by the Spirit of God. First Corinthians 2:14 describes the state of a person who does not have the Spirit: "The person without the Spirit does not accept the things that come from the Spirit of God but considers them foolishness, and cannot understand them because they are discerned only through the Spirit." Here are some typical phrases a spiritually dead person might say:

- I don't believe there's a God.
- Christianity is just one of many paths.
- The Bible is an unreliable book that can't be trusted.
- Religion is a crutch for the weak.
- Christians are hypocritical, intolerant, and hateful people.

When the Holy Spirit begins to awaken a heart to God's Word, and people respond to the gospel, the spiritually dead can be born again (John 3:3–5), regardless of what they've done, where they've been, or the ungodly doubt they've harbored. Jesus is gracious, specializing in redeeming broken lives and resurrecting dead faith.

1. INFANT—LACKING KNOWLEDGE

Once a person has placed their faith in Christ and experienced a new spiritual birth, they have new spiritual taste buds. The Bible may have been a dead, boring book before. Now they are hungry to read it and learn! Spiritual infants need spiritual food. The writer of Hebrews refers to this when he challenges the readers of his letter, telling them that they were still spiritual infants, drinking milk, when they should already be teachers, eating solid food for the mature (Heb. 5:12–14). Spiritual infants tend to lack knowledge about what Jesus really said about life. They are uninformed (not unintelligent) and are in need of truth about God, the world, and themselves.

Years ago, my (Bobby's) wife built a relationship with a woman who became a good friend.

The relationship started out slowly, as they walked together. Then my wife learned that this woman was a Christian. She struggled through a season of trials and difficulties, and this led her to begin coming to church sporadically. Over time she let Cindy more deeply into her life.

> The church is not a theological classroom. It is a conversion, confession, repentance, reconciliation, forgiveness and sanctification center, where flawed people place their faith in Christ, gather to know and love him better, and learn to love others as he designed.
>
> —PAUL TRIPP

This woman said that she was a Christian, and we believe she has trusted Jesus. But she has been poorly discipled. She knew little of what the Bible teaches. There were major areas where she had not surrendered to Jesus as her Lord. She was not married, and she spent time with men in immoral behavior, without realizing that this behavior was a serious problem with God (Gal. 5:19–21) and not good for her children.

How could my wife love her? She started with a nonjudgmental attitude, remembering that her friend did not know any better; she was a spiritual infant who needed love, direction, support, and coaching.

> Maturing in Christ takes time. There is no way that children can be raised in a hurry. To try to get it over quickly can only lead to frustration. The hectic way that churches have tried to force this into a few weeks of confirmation classes, if they have done it at all, is entirely inadequate. Disciples must have devoted Christian friends to follow, and this can only be facilitated by being together over a period of time.
>
> —ROBERT COLEMAN

When people are spiritual infants, their words and actions reveal the truth of who they are. You often hear one or more of the following from infants:

- Jesus, Allah, Buddha, and Karma all express the same principles.
- I had no idea the Bible said that.
- Tithing? What's that?
- I don't really have time for church, and I don't really have to be that involved.

Think about a newborn baby and its needs. To grow and thrive, babies need someone to feed and care for them. In the same way, spiritual infants require the personal attention of a disciple maker, a spiritual parent. They need care and protection during this vulnerable stage. They need the truths of the Christian faith to be taught and modeled to them with love and joy. And they need to develop new habits that form new life patterns.

2. CHILD—SELF-CENTERED, BUT GROWING

In 1 Thessalonians 2:10–12, Paul described himself as a spiritual father dealing with his children, encouraging, comforting, and urging them to live lives worthy of God. People in the "child" stage are growing in their relationship with God and beginning to grow in their relationships with other Christians. But like all children, they are naturally self-centered.

A few years ago I (Bobby) entered into a discipling relationship with a younger man in our church. As I admitted in the last chapter, sometimes I have lacked discernment in who I have recruited and invested my time in—and

I invited this man into a discipleship group because I liked him and we shared an interest in sports. We started meeting together with several other men early in the morning for breakfast before we went to work. He began growing in his knowledge, opening up to the others in the group, and making good strides as a disciple. He had been a Christian for years, but no one had ever discipled him, so he was naturally childish.

He kept telling me that he was really enjoying the group. Then one day, out of the blue, he told me that he was leaving the church and quitting our group. There was no discussion, he said nothing to me or to the other guys. Nothing was processed—that was it. So I called him. "Help me to understand what's happening," I said. He didn't say much, just a few shallow reasons why they were leaving. "My wife decided she didn't like a couple of things at the church, so we are just going to find another one." I still didn't understand. "We have been meeting regularly for months," I said. "Do you not want to talk about this a little bit?" "I love our meetings," he said, "but I want my wife to be happy. What makes her happy, makes me happy." He was like a child. He didn't see the decision to leave as a big deal, like leaving behind his spiritual family. It was more like a game. He picked up his ball and joined his wife to play at somebody else's house.

I shouldn't have been surprised. Spiritual children are like that. We need to be careful that we avoid becoming judgmental when spiritual children act like children. It is natural for a Christian to process through a childhood phase on the way to becoming a spiritual young adult or parent. We need to challenge this behavior, but we do this with love and grace. Some will respond to our guidance and direction. Others will not.

Remember, when we understand that growth as a disciple is a journey and a process, we can have appropriate expectations of those we are discipling. At this stage you might hear someone say:

- My church isn't feeding me.
- I would love to serve more, but I don't have time.
- My small group is about to multiply, and I'm not okay with that.
- I can't believe God would allow such pain to occur in my life.

People in this stage of growth need to learn to do the right things for the right reasons no matter how they feel. This is where a person will begin to experience some growth pains and may at first be tempted to avoid pain or conflict. They may be emotionally immature as well. Discipling someone involves modeling maturity and teaching them to cultivate a servant's heart rather than a self-centered one.

As a person is leaving the child stage of spiritual development, he or she will develop more of a biblical worldview—making decisions more and more through the eyes and mind of Jesus. They will also show signs of emotional maturity—how to identify their own motives, confess their sins, confront others with love, and speak and receive truth without growing defensive. Growing in grace, they will begin to see accountability from others as a good thing, something they need to help them become a mature follower of Christ. Instead of being threatened by others, they will invite them more deeply into their lives.

3. YOUNG ADULT—FOCUSED ON GOD'S KINGDOM

First John 2:13–14 describes those who are spiritual young men. They have overcome the evil one, and the Word of God abides in them. Spiritual young adults are recognizable because they are making a shift from being self-centered to being God-centered and others-centered. It is a joy to disciple people in this stage of spiritual development. The Spirit is transforming their hearts, and the kingdom of God is becoming the most important thing to them.

A man in one of my (Josh) discipleship groups recently faced a major decision affecting his future. He has a real heart for God and his kingdom and regularly signs up to serve in the church. He has expressed a willingness to do whatever he can to help us with our mission. He was offered a very prestigious job at a much higher rate of pay in another city. He was so excited because he was being offered his dream job. We prayed together about the move. I thought he would move. But then something happened.

The more this man and his wife prayed about the decision, the more they started to see how it would impact their effectiveness in the things of God. If they moved, it would hurt several key ministries in the church. They would lose important discipling relationships in their family. If they moved, they would be shrinking back from God's priorities in their lives. They called to tell me that he was not going to accept the job. I was blown away by their spiritual maturity.

> Because you have been created by God as a unique person, his plan to grow you will not look the same as his plan to grow anyone else. What would grow an orchid would drown a cactus.
>
> —JOHN ORTBERG

Wow! People who spiritually develop like these folks make a big difference for Christ in the world. You might hear these phrases from someone in the young adult stage:

- I feel compelled to pray for my neighbor who doesn't know Jesus.
- I really want to make a difference for God. Maybe I can serve in the soup kitchen downtown.
- I wonder what I can do to help my church.
- Bill and Sue missed our group, so I called them to see if they're okay.
- I feel good about the money we give back to God, and I am glad to do my part.

Spiritual young adults need help identifying their gifts. And they need ongoing skills training. It is also easy for a young adult to revert back to the childhood stage. A critical and defining issue at this stage is unexpected hardship and difficulty. When it happens, they need to process the pain so that they don't become disillusioned and cynical. They may also have lingering sin struggles that Satan utilizes to keep them from feeling secure enough in their spiritual maturity to invest in other people.

My (Josh) friend John is a good example of how this can happen. John became a disciple of Jesus as a high school student. He attended church services and participated in his youth group, but no one ever showed him *how* to trust and follow Jesus in a safe, relational environment. John was becoming a spiritual adult, influencing others. But he had a sin problem. One of the ways John learned to cope with stress and unresolved pain from the past was to look at Internet pornography. This sin was especially appealing to him when he was lonely, frustrated, or tired. It seemed as if every time he started to make big strides, difficulties would arise. When they did, he'd often fall again and return to porn.

His wife was aware of his sin, and one day she decided that she had had enough. She packed her things, loaded their two young daughters in the car, and drove away. John called me as she was driving off. He was devastated. I walked him through some key Scriptures on repentance (like Psalm 51) and encouraged him to formulate a repentance plan—based on our belief that true repentance requires a good plan, a healthy process, and relational accountability. He brought that plan to the men's group he was a part of and asked his brothers to hold him accountable.

Several months later, John and his wife were reconciled and are more connected than ever before. He now serves as a small group leader where he disciples men who want to break free from their own sinful prisons.

4. PARENT—INTENTIONAL DISCIPLE MAKERS

Once people are effectively discipled, a mark of maturity is that they can repeat the process with others. Spiritual parents make disciples because they want to love God with everything they've got, and they love people as they love themselves. They know there is nothing more loving a person can do for others than to inspire them to follow Jesus. Second Timothy 2:1–2 describes people who are strong in the grace that is in Christ Jesus. They are reliable disciples who have developed to the point where they are qualified to teach others.

We made this point in an earlier chapter, but it is so important we are going to make it again: the distinguishing mark of a spiritual parent who makes disciples is *intentionality*. Like young adults who focus on God's kingdom, spiritual parents do the same but take it a step further—by investing themselves strategically in the lives of others as disciple makers.

Think about it. If Jesus' mission was to seek and save the lost and to make disciples, how could those becoming most like him not have that as their mission? What was more central to Jesus than making disciples? Likewise, what could be a better sign of true Christlike formation than doing what Jesus did?

One of our elders stands out strongly in this regard. A couple of years ago we asked our elders—who are wise, godly men involved in discipling communities—to move more intentionally into discipling relationships with other men. Ted (not his real name) took our encouragement to heart. Ted is an introvert, so he preferred one-on-one meetings. He started to regularly meet for coffee with certain men in the church who had leadership potential. Now, when we travel around, we regularly find him in coffee shops meeting with these men. He studies the Bible with them, coaches them, and guides them. When any of them run into difficulties or uncertainties in life, he is the first one to whom they turn. He is an intentional disciple maker, making disciples in keeping with his God-given personality.

The following statements characterize the parent stage:

> The most important task of your life is not what you do, but who you become.
>
> —JOHN ORTBERG

- I wonder if God is leading me to invest in Bill and to help him mature in his faith.
- I am burdened for this guy at work. He asked me to explain the Bible to him. Pray for me as I spend time in the Word with him.

- I am so happy that we get to baptize Jane in our small group tonight!
- The most important discipleship is with my kids. I need encouragement and accountability so that I make it a priority.
- I may be the most important person to influence my grandchildren for Jesus. I wonder how I can disciple them.

"Parents" need someone to disciple them in disciple making. They already have a heart for God. They need practical models, easy-to-use tools, and reproducible systems. They also need encouragement and ongoing training to help sharpen and hone their skills. The hallmark of a spiritual parent is a God-given desire to reproduce—to leverage their influence to help others to trust and follow Jesus.

5. GRANDPARENT—MULTIPLYING DISCIPLE MAKERS

Jesus' original intent is that his disciples would make disciples who would make disciples—with a multiplying movement that reaches into every people group on the earth (Matt. 28:19–20). The book of Revelation pictures Jesus' mission as a reality:

After this I looked, and there before me was a great multitude that no one could count, from every nation, tribe, people and language, standing before the throne and before the Lamb. They were wearing white robes and were holding palm branches in their hands. (Rev. 7:9)

This vision is that which motivates those who become spiritual grandparents. With God's help and empowerment, they have multiplied their disciple-making efforts well beyond themselves to people they do not directly disciple themselves.

In 2 Timothy 2:2 the apostle Paul encourages Timothy to become a spiritual grandparent, as Paul is a spiritual grandparent:

And the things you have heard me say in the presence of many witnesses entrust to reliable people who will also be qualified to teach others.

So Timothy is directed by Paul, not just to disciple reliable people; Timothy is to entrust the teaching he received (from Paul) to reliable people, so they can teach others. Paul actually pictures disciple making to the fourth generation in this text: Paul is a great-grandparent, who helps Timothy to become a grandparent, who helps parents (reliable people) to disciple others!

In many ways, this is an ideal picture for those who are in part-time or full-time ministry, as a part of a disciple-making church. We make disciples, but even more: we devote much of our time to making disciple makers who make disciples. At this level the influence and impact of our ministry extends beyond our direct influence. We move from adding people whom we disciple (spiritual parent) to multiplying disciple makers (spiritual grandparent).

The following statements characterize the grandparent stage:

- I am praying that God will show me whom I should invest in and raise up to be disciple makers in this next season.
- I am so happy to hear that Michelle is going to baptize another person from the group that she is leading; that was our dream when I first started meeting with her a few years ago!
- I'm overwhelmed with thankfulness when I find out about people—who I do not personally know—who have been raised up to become disciple makers, by disciple makers that I do know.
- My biggest joy is when I hear about multiple generations of disciple makers who were influenced by those I was blessed to disciple and influence.
- I look forward to hearing from Jason; I am excited to hear about who God is using him to reach in the disciple-making works he has started since we sent him out.

Bobby's friend Ralph Moore is an ordinary guy. He is not a polished speaker, and he is not a master strategist. He just loves God and does his best to make disciples through a simple, reproducible process.

> Jesus matters because of what he brought and what he still brings to ordinary human beings, living their ordinary lives and coping daily with their surroundings. He promises wholeness for their lives. In sharing our weaknesses he gives us strength and imparts through his companionship a life that has the quality of eternity.
>
> —DALLAS WILLARD

Yet Ralph is the best example we can find of a spiritual grandparent. He started the Hope Chapel movement with a focus on making disciples who make disciples. As Ralph kept sending out those he had discipled to go and plant disciple-making churches, they kept the disciple-making DNA going. They made disciples who made disciples who planted churches that planted churches. And on and on they have been going. That movement now has well over 2,350 churches that have been planted since the early 1970s. It is a great, inspirational picture of a kingdom movement! Ralph shows us that God can do extraordinary things through ordinary people. If you are reading this book, that likely applies to you, just like it does to us.

PAUSE AND PONDER

Where would you locate yourself on the spiritual growth chart?

We want to close by reiterating something we said earlier. The real-life journey of spiritual growth is unpredictable and difficult at times. More often than not, the path is more circular than linear. And it requires more than Bible knowledge, supportive relationships with other Christians, and service. Disciple makers must remember that this path inevitably brings suffering and persecution. There will be times of confusion, stumbling in and out of sin (with repentance), and both regressive and progressive steps (sometimes simultaneously). The work you do will be opposed by the enemy, and you will need to utilize spiritual weapons of prayer and God's Word to defeat the lies and attacks of the evil one. Parents have a need for constant and ongoing encouragement and love and reminders of God's grace.

We must remember that our God is "compassionate and gracious, slow to anger, abounding in love" (Ps. 103:8). The people you disciple will need gentle reminders that God's grace fuels our obedience and devotion to him. They will not only need to hear about grace, but need to experience it firsthand from you.

A person can progress at one level through the steps in a few years, but then regress backward. No one travels a straight journey. It is a lifelong process. None of us arrive until the final grand conclusion of history (Revelation 21).

HOW DO WE APPLY THIS TODAY?

The first practical way to implement this element into our discipleship is to acknowledge the fact that everyone is on a journey with God. While it is impossible to know exactly where a person is with the Lord, we all need guidance from others who will help us examine ourselves accurately.

A word of advice. Based on our experience, we don't think it is healthy or effective to tell someone where they are in terms of their spiritual development. Ideally, the people you're investing in would want to assess their own spiritual maturity in a biblical way. Some will need more coaching than others with this.

We recommend that you ask God to sharpen your ability to discern a person's spiritual condition. Pray for God to enable you to see beyond the ordinary, outward life we live. This begins, of course, with you practicing the discipline of self-examination and, as a result, growing in self-awareness. The better you know your own soul, the more able you'll be to know theirs.

- Everyone has a distinct life story and journey with God.
- We should spend more time and energy examining our own lives than looking at the lives of others.
- The Holy Spirit is able to help you see where a person is with the Lord and empower you to meet them in that place and guide them appropriately.
- After you earn the right to be heard, don't be passive about speaking into someone's life. Speak the truth in love.
- Resist the urge to push or make something happen for someone. You are not the Holy Spirit! Your job is to love and equip. It's the Spirit's to convict and change.

FOR REFLECTION AND CONVERSATION

1. What are the three different roles in a disciple-making relationship, and why is it important for the disciple maker to have a clear sense of the responsibilities in each role?

2. How thorough is your knowledge of the discipleship journey? Why is it important to know and understand the basic discipleship journey?

3. What are the five stages of the discipleship journey as the Bible lays it out?

4. What is your intended destination for the person you're discipling along the discipleship pathway? Why is it important to think "next stage" or "next steps" rather than the "entire journey"?

5. How does your life journey mesh with the journey of the person you're discipling?

Chapter 10

MULTIPLY

> And the things you have heard me say in the
> presence of many witnesses entrust to reliable
> people who will also be qualified to teach others.
>
> 2 TIMOTHY 2:2

Before we jump into this chapter, take a moment to read the passage above one more time . . . slowly. Analyze it. Look at it phrase by phrase. We see this as one of the key passages in the Bible on multiplication. Why? It speaks of four generations of disciples and disciple making: Paul (the one writing); his disciple, Timothy (the person he is writing to); the "reliable people" Timothy will teach in his church; and those "others," the people who will teach about Jesus and his ways. Everything we've said about intentionality is summed up in this one little verse. It is a beautiful picture of how multiplication works.

When the apostle Paul describes how he equipped Timothy as a disciple maker, he writes about the multiplication process. Not long after he wrote what we just read, he recalls what it was like for Timothy to learn from him.

> You, however, know all about my teaching, my way of life, my purpose, faith, patience, love, endurance, persecutions, sufferings—what kinds of things

happened to me in Antioch, Iconium and Lystra, the persecutions I endured. . . . But as for you, continue in what you have learned and have become convinced of, because you know those from whom you learned it (2 Tim. 3:10–11, 14).

This passage describes the kind of intentional discipleship that I (Bobby) received that helped me to become a spiritual parent and church leader. At age twenty-nine, I became the senior pastor/minister of an older established church, and the church had a semi-retired minister on staff named Cecil. He and his wife, Levine, were wonderful people, and they took my wife and me under their wings. They invited us into their world. Though they never stated it outright, they patterned their discipleship after Paul's example in 2 Timothy 3.

> The apostle Paul worked this way. He devoted large amounts of time, he followed up, backtracked, and he arranged for others to be with his disciples.
>
> —ROBERT COLEMAN

I fondly remember how they took us with them on a road trip to meet all the leaders they knew within our fellowship of churches. Over the months and years that we worked together, they regularly had us over for supper, lunch, or for a "cup of tea" (older Canadians love "having tea"). We laughed, cried, and disagreed with each other about important things. We got to know their children, their grandchildren, and their way of life. We learned their stories of persecution and suffering in ministry. Their friendship made us stronger and wiser in our own faith and prepared us for the years of ministry that lay ahead. They loved us and discipled us.

I still smile after all these years recalling some of our conversations. I remember the time we had a "huge" problem at the church—people blocking our plans as leaders. I went to Cecil because I did not know what to do. I assumed he would tell me to be patient and just wait it out a few years. Honestly, if he had said to back down, I would have done it. But he surprised me with a vision for the future instead. "Well," he said to me, "we just have to figure out how to ram it through!" I didn't expect him to say that. But he understood that there are times when you can't be a peacemaker. You have to fight for what you know is right. Cecil taught me that there are times when you need to risk the conflict. He knew that the opportunity we had for growth at that stage might not come up again in this generation, and we needed to show some decisive leadership.

I learned to be a leader from this experience with Cecil and am forever indebted to him and his wife for their care and wisdom.

Cecil and his wife passed along what they knew about God to my wife and me. He was intentional in discipling us to maturity. Again, let's look at Paul's instructions to Timothy in 2 Timothy 2:2:

> The things you have heard me say in the presence of many witnesses entrust to reliable people who will also be qualified to teach others.

Timothy was to take the principles Paul had taught him and entrust them to reliable people. He was to exercise wisdom and discernment in how he applied this strategy because he was instructed to discern and teach it to *reliable people*. It was a clear discipleship strategy. Additionally, Paul was strategic and careful with both his life and his doctrine, for both are indispensable parts in the discipleship process (1 Tim. 4:16). We think it is very important to delineate the discipleship Paul is talking about and a kind of discipleship that is often practiced today—the difference between *intentional, relational* discipleship and *classroom* (or educational) discipleship. Far too many people think of discipleship as teaching the Bible or a download of Bible facts. Teaching and doctrine are important, but as we have previously emphasized, focusing on Bible knowledge is too narrow in scope to capture what Jesus and the apostles practiced.

Discipleship in the Bible is life on life, heart with heart, eyeball to eyeball. Paul was as concerned about how he lived in front of Timothy, how he modeled the faith and how he showed Timothy how to lead, as he was concerned with doctrine. Again, it was life and doctrine working in tandem—both are equally important. Disciple makers who multiply disciples hold equally to both parts of this tension.

---

1. CULTIVATE THE RIGHT HEART.

We have been emphasizing the key role of intentionality in multiplication and in being a spiritual parent, but there is one other aspect that must be mentioned. The source of our intentionality is our motive and desire. It is the heart of a disciple maker, the heart of a spiritual parent. To have intentionality without the heart that Jesus had for disciple making is like having a car without an engine. That person will not go anywhere. Before we become disciple makers, an awakening must occur within our hearts. And once our hearts have been awakened, we need to cultivate desire for Jesus and a love for others.

The heart of a disciple maker must be transformed. First, we must come to the point where we desire to truly love God and love people. We must experientially learn what it means to die to ourselves. The Holy Spirit transitions us from *me* to *ministry*. We are freed from the slavery of self-absorption. This is what it means to love God and love people the way Jesus did.

> Success should be measured not by how many disciples are made, but by how many disciples are making other disciples.
>
> —BILL HULL

Jesus knew his Father better than anyone. He knew what pleased the Father and how to live in a way that brought honor to God. He lived an obedient, holy, and sinless life. Jesus always did the right thing, and he always did it for the right reason. Every single time. He was human as humans were created to be. He worshiped full-heartedly, prayed humbly, studied the Bible rigorously, went to synagogue consistently, observed the Sabbath religiously, honored his mother and father unwaveringly . . . you get the point. But notice that because he loved God perfectly, he was also able to love people perfectly.

Jesus did not come into this world and go to the cross with his eyes fixed *on* us. Jesus went to the cross *for* us with his eyes fixed *on* God (Matt. 26:39; Heb. 12:2–3). His perfect love for the Father expressed itself in sacrificial love for people. And his love for God and people led Jesus to seek and save the lost (Luke 19:9–10). Love for God and people led Jesus to make disciples (John 13:34–35).

A true disciple wants to be just like Jesus. A true disciple wants to be a disciple of Jesus who makes disciples, like Jesus did. The development of a heart like this in our lives, one that truly loves God, loves people, and denies self is the result of a Spirit-fueled maturation process.

When Jesus took his disciples to the district of Caesarea Philippi, it was a crucial turning point and a new phase in Jesus' disciple-making ministry.[1] This area is in the northern part of Israel, a pagan region away from the Jewish crowds that followed him. Jesus took his disciples up there to help them understand their need for a heart change, one that they would need to eventually make to become authentic disciples and disciple makers. Mark describes this turning point in Mark 8:27, 29:

> Jesus and his disciples went on to the villages around Caesarea Philippi. On the way he asked them, "Who do people

say I am?" . . . Peter answered, "You are the Messiah."

Two things happened at this place. First, Jesus presses the disciples with a fundamentally important coaching question on his identity. He wants them to see something that is fundamental to his mission. Peter answers his question correctly, responding that he is the Messiah (the Christ). Mark then records something essential that Jesus wants his disciples to know and process (8:31–33):

He then began to teach them that the Son of Man must suffer many things and be rejected by the elders, the chief priests and the teachers of the law, and that he must be killed and after three days rise again. He spoke plainly about this, and Peter took him aside and began to rebuke him. But when Jesus turned and looked at his disciples, he rebuked Peter. "Get behind me, Satan!" he said. "You do not have in mind the concerns of God, but merely human concerns."

Jesus explains that, as God's Messiah, he is going to suffer and be killed. That does not square with Peter's concept of the kingdom or of the Messiah. But Jesus strongly rebukes him, saying that he does not have the right mind-set on this matter. Following that encounter, Jesus makes a second key point about disciples and disciple makers in the next two verses (Mark 8:34–35):

Then he called the crowd to him along with his disciples and said: "Whoever wants to be my disciple must deny themselves and take up their cross and follow me. For whoever wants to save their life will lose it, but whoever loses their life for me and for the gospel will save it."

Jesus has just described his mission as the Messiah; he will soon suffer and die on the cross. And here, near the end of his earthly ministry, he says that the *willingness to die to yourself* is the distinguishing mark of spiritual maturation. During this last phase of his ministry to the disciples, Jesus repeatedly emphasized the need to deny self and live for others (Mark 9:31–32; 10:32–34). The Last Supper and garden of Gethsemane prior to his crucifixion also magnify this point (John 13:1–38). Jesus serves his disciples and models what it is to forgo one's selfish desires for the kingdom. Jesus tells them that they should become like him. Again, a person cannot truly become a healthy disciple maker or truly live life in light of the gospel until he or she dies to themselves and surrenders his or her dreams for life to God.

The death of the self describes the process of transformation. We die to ourselves—our sinful orientation to self—and come alive each day to the Spirit of God and our new life in Christ. This process of dying leads to a fundamental change of heart. It may involve leaving a successful career or giving up a privileged position. It may mean the death of a dream, and instead put the needs of another before your own. And while such dying is painful, Jesus promises us joy. After all, it was joy that led him to the cross: "For the joy set before him [Christ] endured the cross, scorning its shame" (Heb. 12:2).

> You and I can choose to continue with business as usual in the Christian life and in the church as a whole, enjoying success based on the standards defined by the culture around us. Or we can take an honest look at the Jesus of the Bible and dare to ask what the consequences might be if we really believed him and really obeyed him.
>
> —DAVID PLATT

I (Josh) have a friend who experienced this heart shift shortly after he graduated (with honors) with his MBA. He was not only well-educated, he was a natural-born leader with innate gifts and instincts for influencing and persuading others. His career path was packed with promises of promotions, luxury, and wealth. But that all changed after he took a trip to a Third World city in Honduras. As hard as he tried, he couldn't un-see what he saw there . . . and he couldn't un-feel what he felt as he witnessed extreme poverty and its multilayered pain. He told me that it was like Jesus was whispering in his ear, "There's a better life available to you than the one you've planned out. Come with me and let me show you how to live according to your original design." He followed that still, small voice, and he used his great talent and education to plant churches and start businesses in Honduras. The operation he leads is called "Mission Lazarus"—he and his wife and many others who've joined them devote their lives to helping people experience radical resurrection.

And they're so full of joy! Have you ever noticed that the happiest people are also the most selfless? That jolt of joy we get when we give ourselves away for the sake of others is the smile of God himself.

A disciple maker will continue to battle with selfish desires. Not one of us is perfect. But growing as a disciple maker is all about dying to self. If we resist this, we will tend to use other people or instill in them truths about being a disciple that are reflections of our wisdom and not God's truth. A person who has truly surrendered and died to their dreams for the sake of God's calling is a very effective disciple maker. They do this because they love God, not to prove themselves or build their kingdom. They now live for God's kingdom. It is now about other people, not themselves.

- Pray for emerging disciple makers as Jesus prayed for Peter (Luke 22:31–32).
- Help emerging disciple makers to see that hardships refine and purify our faith (Rom. 5:3–5).
- In love and in close relationship, help those you are discipling to work through the heart change of the death-to-self challenge.
- Help people see that those who best love God and love people have died to themselves so that Jesus lives through them (Gal. 2:20).
- See them become who God—not the world—calls them to be.

2. MAKE THE METHOD EASILY REPRODUCIBLE.

Those who become spiritual parents will express a desire to become disciple makers themselves if they have been trained (Luke 6:40). We should walk closely with those we send out as we fully release them. New disciple makers will continue to need support and help from other disciple makers. In truth, we never stop needing encouragement and support.

> God has always been interested in reproduction. If fact, His first command to Adam and Eve in the Garden was not to be spiritual, productive, or upstanding citizens of earth. Rather, it was to "be fruitful and multiply" (Genesis 1:28).
>
> —ROBBY GALLATY

There are three tangible elements that enable everyday disciples to become disciple makers: *a tool, a plan, and a process*. They need tools that are simple enough so most people can use them. They need a plan, even if it is a flexible plan. And they need a reproducible process so that they can gauge their progress with the tools and plan.

Tools: As we described in the chapter on intentionality, disciple makers need tools. The tools help them to lead other disciples on the discipleship path. The tools guide, teach, and direct the disciple in the journey toward Jesus and Christlikeness. The tool you use might be as simple as *Discovery Bible Study*, a simple and open Bible-study format with specialized questions and encouragement to fast and pray and find a person of peace (those uniquely able to open doors to expanding relationships). Or it could be an eight-part Bible study that everyone in the church goes through to ensure that they have committed themselves to Jesus and the path of discipleship. Or it might be more complex, like the in-depth life-on-life studies created by Perimeter Church in Atlanta. Each church will need to clarify its "go-to tools."

Plan: There is an old saying that bears repeating here: *Those who fail to plan, plan to fail.* Disciple makers need to understand how to use the tools that have been developed by the church or ministry. Like tools, the discipleship plans that can be utilized are diverse. Tools and plans go hand in hand. In fact, an important part of effectiveness is coupling tools and plans so that they work well together. In this way, disciple makers know where they are going and the plan to get there.

Process: Both conversion and sanctification (growth in Christlikeness) are processes, with traceable, discernible steps. Disciple makers need to understand the process behind the plan. This enables them to be patient with those they are discipling. Just as coaches need to know how to plan the game and how to win so they can coach their players, so the disciple maker needs to know the growth process to coach the disciple.

The process will have micro-steps. For example, the first step in our church to helping a non-Christian to consider the claims of Jesus is to develop a relationship with them. Once the relationship has been established, we encourage our people to invite folks into a Bible study, a home group, or a church service. These relational environments then lead to understanding the Bible, understanding the gospel, and so forth. We are always developing tools to help guide people through these micro-steps.

I (Josh) am grateful for a tool we use with people who express interest in becoming followers of Jesus. It's a simple four-part booklet that explains the biblical teachings of repentance (turning from sin) and faith (turning toward Jesus). It was just the tool I needed during a conversation I was having with my friend John. Our kids were in the same class at school, and I'm praying all the time for Jesus to open doors and forge connections with people who are open to him. I had been hanging out a lot with John—drinking coffee, sharing meals, lots of small talk. At some point, he started asking questions about my relationship with Jesus and then started attending our weekend church gatherings. He had grown up going to church, but it sounded more like an empty social club than a vibrant community of faith.

After several weeks, the Jesus switch was

flipped in his heart, and I got to be there when it happened. I walked him through the brochure. We read the Scripture passages together. He raised countless questions and wanted to process everything, which is good. The tool we developed was designed for conversations just like that one. Anyone can use it. And by using it, anyone in our church can lead others to surrender their lives to Jesus.

Here are several questions you should think through and review with others as you consider becoming a disciple maker:

- What tool will you use?
- How well do you understand the tool?
- What is the plan you will follow with your disciple?
- What is the process and end goal you have for your disciple?
- How well do you understand the plan and process?

3. CULTIVATE INTENTIONALITY AND SKILL.

Disciple makers don't just happen; they are made. They are people who have themselves been discipled. When we are intentional, what we do is more likely to be repeatable. We like the way Jim Putman says this—*That which is unintentional is not reproducible.* We are not just making disciples, but disciples who will mature to become disciple makers.

Our friends Dave and Jon Ferguson have a helpful formula they use and teach to describe the process of intentional discipleship. This formula describes the ideal mind-set of a disciple maker and what it means to be committed to repeating the discipleship process.[2]

- I do. You watch. We talk.
- I do. You help. We talk.
- You do. I help. We talk.
- You do. I watch. We talk.
- You do. Someone else watches. I do. Someone else watches.

We have found this simple description easy to memorize and easy to practice. When I (Bobby) am discipling a small group leader, I follow the pattern it describes and teach them the formula. Consider my friend Kevin, for example. I was leading a small group, and he was my apprentice. So we started with the first phase. I would lead the group, and then afterward, on the phone as we were driving home, we would talk about everything that happened in the group that night.

Before long, I was getting Kevin to help me.

Because I was intentional with him, we would plan it out before the meeting. "Kevin, would you lead the retelling of the story?" I might say. Then, after the group was over, we would talk. Finally, Kevin was leading the group, and I was watching and debriefing. He eventually moved on to lead his own group. We had followed the process.

This kind of explicit, intentional guidance is not optional. Kevin was equipped to lead a group, but we also equipped him with an intentional disciple-making strategy that he can now use with others. Remember, Jesus had a master plan. Jesus was intentional. He executed a strategy with absolute precision. He knew exactly what he was doing. In the process, he raised up disciple-making leaders who ignited a movement that has spread throughout the world.

- Tell those you are discipling that you are preparing them to disciple others.
- Be explicitly intentional with your disciples about why you do what you do—so they can replicate it.
- The clearer you are, the clearer it will be to those you are discipling, and the clearer they will be as disciple makers.
  - What is a biblical disciple?
  - What is the discipleship process?
  - What is God's part, what is my part, what is your part?

- The discipleship journey is unfinished until the people you're discipling are discipling others.
- Disciple making is the calling and responsibility of every Christian, not just church leaders.

4. MAINTAIN PASSION FOR THE MISSION.

Sometimes the barrier to multiplication is not lack of skill or a usable process. We just need to be reminded of the mission. We know that our mission is to make disciples who make disciples . . . but our passion can wane. This is normal and it can be overcome. We need to constantly encourage and exhort one another. We need to fan the flames of passion for lost people and immature disciples. The apostle Paul perfectly described the mind-set in 1 Corinthians 9:19–22:

Though I am free and belong to no one, I have made myself a slave to everyone, to win as many as possible. To the Jews I became like a Jew, to win the Jews. To those under the law I became like one under the law (though I myself am not under the law), so as to win those under the law. To those not having the law I became like one not having the law (though I am not free from God's law but am under Christ's law), so as to win those not having the law. To the weak I became weak, to win the weak. I have become all things to all people so that by all possible means I might save some.

Disciple making, as we have said throughout, is something we do with lost people and with Christians. It requires our best efforts. Countless numbers of lost people will never be saved without it. And countless numbers of Christians will never overcome sin patterns and barriers to growth without the help of a disciple maker.

How do you cultivate passion? It helps if you surround yourself with people who share your passion. Do you have a passion for lost people? Get around other people who love the lost and encourage one another. Spend time reading about Jesus and how he went after the lost and made it his mission to reach them. It also helps to listen to preaching that reminds us of eternal truth. For example, we don't always hear much about hell in churches anymore.

We tend to gravitate away from passages and truths that teach us about God's holiness and lead us to respect and fear the Lord, preferring truths that emphasize the love of God. But the Bible says we need both and that they are different sides of the same truth. The fear of God is the beginning of wisdom (Prov. 1:7). Learning to see the holiness of God and the consequences of sin expands our awareness of God's love in saving us from our sin. We stand amazed at his mercy, and our love for him and others increases. Over time, we will become confident of our eternal destiny (Rom. 8:39), but we never lose our sense of awe and wonder at our salvation.

As with anything, it is easy to lose balance. This is why we need to keep biblical truth before us, regularly studying all the Scriptures and not just the parts we like. Hell is real and people are going there (Matt. 7:13–14). Lost people will not turn to Christ unless they first become convinced that they are lost. As we grow in maturity, we begin to see how the kindness and sternness of God work together toward one purpose—our growth into the likeness of Christ (Rom. 11:22). God is love (1 John 4:16), and God's love is a holy love (1 Peter 1:15–16).

Tony Campolo used to tell an insightful story about the death of Charlie Peace in London in 1854. Charlie was sentenced to be hung by the prison authorities, and at that time the Anglican church had a ceremony for criminals who were about to be hung. A church leader was reading to Charlie from the Prayer Book:

"Those who die without Christ experience hell, which is the pain of forever dying without the release which death itself can bring." When these chilling words were read, Charlie Peace stopped in his tracks, turned to the priest, and shouted in his face, "Do you believe that? Do you believe that?" The priest, taken aback by this sudden verbal assault, stammered for a moment and then said, "Well . . . I . . . suppose I do." "Well, I don't," said Charlie. "But if I did, I'd get down on my hands and knees and crawl all over Great Britain, even if it were paved with pieces of broken glass, if I could just rescue one person from what you just told me."[3]

Far too many of us have lost an awareness of what it really means to be eternally lost. Because we do not truly grasp the reality of hell, we do not have strong convictions about how essential it is that we help everyone we can to come to Jesus Christ. There have been great leaders who have shown us how God will use someone with a single passion to reach others.

"I look upon this world as a wrecked vessel," D. L. Moody, the great evangelist of the mid-1800s said. "God has given me a lifeboat and said to me, 'Moody, save all you can.'"[4]

At the turn of the last century, Charles Spurgeon said, "It is a grand thing to see a man who is thoroughly possessed with one master passion."[5] Spurgeon also said, "If you think you are going to win souls, you must throw your soul into your work, just as a warrior must throw his soul into a battle, or victory will not be yours. . . . Indeed it is a race. As such, nobody wins unless he strains every muscle and sinew."[6]

Billy Graham, the renowned evangelist of the second half of the twentieth century, summed up his life with these words: "My one purpose in life is to help people find a personal relationship with God."[7] May God give us men and women like that today!

May our convictions about the need to make disciples be strong! Can we say that Jesus really is "the way and the truth and the life" (John 14:6)? Is it true that "no one comes to the Father except through [him]"? Can we say that there is "no other name under heaven . . . by which [people] must be saved" (Acts 4:12)? These are essential convictions if we are to make disciples out of those who do not know Jesus.

Those in our churches need to be discipled as well. The church is filled with immature Christians, infants who have never been taught the basics of the faith. They need help to become the people God wants them to become. They will need relational guidance through each step of the journey, from infancy through childhood through young adulthood and even as spiritual parents. Those who multiply disciples and disciple making have a passion for people and the lordship of Jesus. They want others to be who God wants them to be. God's plan is that we help and guide one another. God wants us to multiply those who are helping people to trust and follow Jesus.

We have a woman in our church who is one of the most effective disciple makers we know. She helps women overcome relationship dependency as a sponsor in our Celebrate Recovery ministry. She joins her husband in leading a small group, and she individually disciples women. Her life is characterized by great passion to be a disciple who makes disciples. She wants women to be all that God wants them to be! So she invests herself every day in helping others trust and follow Jesus.

One of the women she disciples recently spoke up at a public gathering. She described how she was shown love and acceptance by our disciple-making friend. This woman had been a Christian for many years and was herself in ministry for fourteen years, but no one had ever discipled her in how to be victorious over fear. It was crippling her life, and she needed someone to disciple her in this critical area of her life.

It took over a year. They studied the Bible and had many talks and prayers together. Then one day it happened. The fear that had bound her for her entire life had now been replaced by a deeper understanding of God. New habits had been developed (to cope with the underlying issues). She was free! She had been discipled by a woman who loves Jesus and loved her enough to invest in her.

A disciple who was willing to make disciples had changed her life. A child of God experienced the loving touch of her Father, and now she is free to lead others in the freedom she has experienced.

■   ■   ■

Here's the deal. Jesus is not a character in our little stories. We're characters in his grand story. He is under no obligation to help us achieve our goals or advance our personal causes. He has recruited us to participate in his cause of making disciples. If we're wise, we'll get on board with his plan and do it his way. His agenda is unstoppable and his methods are flawless.

One of the surest signs that the Holy Spirit is working in us is that we're asking new questions. These new questions are driven by new desires, and these new desires arise from our union with Jesus.

Old question: How can I live a comfortable life?

New question: How can Jesus help me live a meaningful life?

Old question: What is the path of least resistance?

New question: What does Jesus say is the path of greatest significance?

Old question: What do I want to accomplish today?

New question: Who does Jesus want me to invest in today?

Old question: Life is short—how should I make the most of it?

New question: I will live forever—how can I (with Jesus' help) make an eternal difference?

In the last few years, we've met with several national leaders in the emerging discipleship movement. We have started a new ministry to unite leaders and continue the conversation. You can learn more about this at www.discipleship.org. In starting this ministry, we solicited the input of some the most influential voices in the disciple-making movement in North America and were stunned by their uniform emphasis on one point: *Discipleship is not biblical without an unwavering commitment and emphasis on multiplication.* If our vision of discipleship stops with one disciple, it falls short of the example Jesus left for us. Jesus' goal is for disciples to become disciple makers.

The four gospel accounts make it clear that Jesus wasn't satisfied with just reaching the twelve apostles. After calling, empowering, and instructing them, Jesus sent his disciples out to do ministry. He released them to do what he was doing. Traditional church structures encourage pastors to focus on collecting more and more people. The larger the collection, the more successful the pastor is considered to be. *But Jesus did not collect people. He called and sent them.* The true success of your ministry is not how many people attend your church services, but how many people you have sent out to make disciples.

The litmus test for disciple makers is not whether they are making disciples, but are they making disciples *who have gone on to be disciple makers?* Mature disciple makers can point to the people they have discipled who are now discipling others as co-laborers in Jesus' mission. We may release people from being actively discipled by us, but we never release them from relationship.

- Do your best to make sure that people are both spiritually ready (it is about the kingdom of God) and intellectually ready (they know what to do) before you send them out.
- Pray for them and support them and remind them to rely on God through the Holy Spirit.
- Keep them focused on the basics that disciple making includes an emphasis on baptizing people into Christ and teaching them to obey all of Jesus' teachings.
- Spiritual adults and spiritual parents should be the main focus in this phase.

HOW DO WE APPLY THE ELEMENT OF MULTIPLICATION TODAY?

The first thing you want to do is clarify your motives and your passion. Do you take Jesus at his word, or will you ignore what he has clearly stated? Prepare for opposition if you choose to embrace Jesus' view. It's not popular. It never really has been. Following Jesus isn't about being popular. It's about being faithful.

Remember that the discipleship assignment isn't complete until the people you're investing in are able to make disciples of Jesus on their own.

The Great Commission cannot happen the way Jesus intended until everyday Christians actively participate and stop relying on pastors and church leaders to make disciples.

FOR REFLECTION AND CONVERSATION

1. What is multiplication (of disciples who go on to make other disciples)? Why is it so important that this practice lies at the heart of what it means to make disciples?

2. How does discipleship apply to lost people, and how does this kind of discipleship work in practice?

3. In what way is it Christlike—in light of Luke 15—to go out and find lost people? How can we do that today?

4. In what way is discipleship the ongoing need of all Christians and the core mission of the church?

5. What is the most important thing you have learned from this study, and why is it important to you?

CONCLUSION

Join the Discipleship-First Tribe

You are officially invited to join our tribe! A tribe is a group of distinct people. They can be delineated from others by unique features: beliefs, commitments, values, and lifestyle.

The discipleship-first tribe is unique because it is formed around a core conviction that in turn forms everything else for us. Every day, that core conviction is our dominant thought, our underlying passion in all we think and do. It starts in the morning and guides us until we go to bed at night.

We want to be disciples who make disciples!

We live in light of this core passion—whether we are church planters, businessmen, homemakers, students, pastors, truck drivers, teachers, lawyers, doctors, factory workers, professors, employed doing whatever (or not employed at all)—to trust and follow Jesus and help others to do the same, which is our greatest desire.

Robert Coleman, the father of the modern disciple-making movement, first coined the term "the discipleship lifestyle." That term describes those who belong to our tribe. It is a different way of saying the same thing.

Note this focus: tribe members are fully committed to the two parts of the lifestyle—*being* disciples who *make* disciples. Both parts are essential—being (a disciple of Jesus) leads to doing (making disciples). At the core, discipleship-first people think of themselves in those terms. It is the grand narrative of our lives.

Our world is rapidly changing. We

believe that without the discipleship-first passion, the local church is especially in trouble. We cannot make it today, and the church will slip into greater irrelevance and impotence, without going back to this fundamental commitment from the ministry of Jesus himself.

On a daily basis, more and more Christians are joining us. When we join together, the fires that have been stoked for this grand passion will get stronger. These fires will start others as we pour even more gasoline on them. We believe these fires can ignite a disciple-making movement that will change the church in North America and beyond!

We can do so much more together than we can do separately. With God's assistance, you can help create a stronger and clearer voice. Are you drawn to the discipleship-first tribe? Does something deep within seem to be calling you? It is a choice that only you can make.

As you consider joining the tribe, consider the "drumbeats" listed below. Tribes have distinctive drumbeats, and these three beats most clearly draw us and inextricably lead us to be discipleship-first people. If these convictions excite you, perhaps you are hearing the same drum.

1. IT IS THE ONLY RESPONSE WORTHY OF JESUS.

Jesus is God in the flesh, our Messiah, our savior, our king, our teacher, and our redeemer! Admit it—Jesus' identity and grace and gospel are mind-boggling, almost too good to be true. The only reasonable response is to follow and worship—to form our lives around him, and help others to do the same. Because of who he is and what he has done for us, the discipleship lifestyle is the only worthy response, and because of who Jesus is, nothing is more important than helping others to come to know and embrace him, too. Everything else falls short. There is nothing that honors God and puts Jesus in the right place in a human life more than being a discipleship-first person.

2. IT UPHOLDS JESUS' FINAL COMMAND.

I (Bobby) recently lost my little sister to a terrible brain disease that took her life just six short weeks after the first symptoms appeared. It has been months, and I still have not yet adjusted to losing her. I am moved again, now, just thinking about her loss. In my mind, I keep going over her last words to me and to our family members. I treasure them; they give great meaning to both her life and death.

In a like manner, Jesus' final words should be very important to us. They are formative, giving meaning to his life and death and everything he taught and did. He equipped his disciples to do for others what he had done for them, and then he commissioned them to "go and make disciples of all nations" (Matt. 28:19–20). Their commission is also our commission. It is for every believer and every church—be a disciple and help make disciples.

"Discipleship first" means discipleship is your first impulse. Jesus' last strategic orders are our first order of business. If you truly believe his last words, you have to adjust your life to them.

3. IT IMITATES JESUS AND HIS LOVE.

What does it mean to love like Jesus? Jesus loved God and loved people perfectly. That made him God's perfect disciple. By following him, we learn how to love God and love people. What did he do as he obeyed his Father in all things? He came to seek and save the lost. And he chose to devote the bulk of his time and energy to intentionally and relationally pouring his life into making disciples. He did this to help them love God and love people as he did.

The best way to live life is to model our lives after Jesus' life. Love in the life of Jesus demonstrated itself in his focus on being a disciple who made disciples. May his character and priorities become our character and priorities. Motivated by love and fueled by the Holy Spirit, the result is dramatic transformation. The discipleship lifestyle is simply following the example of Jesus. It is imitating him.

We believe a renewal of the church is at hand, and the rebirth will come through local movements of disciple making that quite literally change the shape of the church and the shape of the world! Discipleship is the hope of the church, and we get to be a part of a new movement that Jesus is stirring up.

You can be a part of it. You can be a disciple who makes disciples. If the ministry of Jesus teaches us anything, it's that anybody—no matter who they are—can become a disciple maker. Will you join the cause? Will you make the decision to become a discipleship-first person? At the end of your life, when we all meet and bow down before Jesus, what else will matter as much?

> Christ with me, Christ before me,
> Christ behind me, Christ in me,
> Christ beneath me, Christ above me,
> Christ on my right, Christ on my left,
> Christ when I lie down, Christ when I
>   sit down,
> Christ when I arise,
> Christ in the heart of every man who
>   thinks of me,
> Christ in the mouth of everyone who
>   speaks of me,
> Christ in every eye that sees me,
> Christ in every ear that hears me.[1]

APPENDIX 1

The DNA of a Disciple-Making Movement

discipleship.org

Imagine a day when Jesus-style disciple making is the norm for the local church. Everyday Christians are engaged in relationships with people (inside and outside the church) so that they can show the love of Jesus and help people to trust and follow him. Churches are known as disciple-making places, where Jesus-like people are created. And pastors are evaluated by the people they raise up and the disciple makers they have made in the Spirit's power. Jesus' message *and* Jesus' methods dominate.

What will it take? We believe that this day will come as God moves among us and as God's people live out certain beliefs. If the following beliefs resonate with you and you can support them, then we hope you will join us.

These beliefs are the DNA of a disciple-making movement.

1. We believe the gospel and it is our message—this good news is focused on Jesus as our Messiah (King) and his death, burial, and resurrection. All who respond to salvation are freely saved and called to discipleship, no exceptions, no excuses (Mark 8:34–38; 1 Cor. 15:1–8). The gospel we preach and believe dictates the kind of disciples we are and the kind of disciples we make. If we attempt to make a Christlike disciple from a non-discipleship gospel, we will fail. A non-discipleship gospel is one that does not include discipleship as a natural part of the message and expectation.

2. We are compelled to be and make disciples of Jesus. We believe Jesus Christ is supreme and worthy of all devotion, worship, and emulation, and disciple making is a natural and necessary life response to Jesus. With laser focus, it was Jesus himself who made disciples who could make disciples . . . and Jesus commands us to do the same (Matt. 28:16–20; John 20:21). We prefer to use the expression "disciple making" over "discipleship" because the former is closer to the words of the Great Commission and the latter is often mischaracterized (Matt. 28:18–20).

3. We believe Jesus is the model (for life and ministry). Jesus showed us how to live life and how to make disciples. We seek to emulate his method and model. As the sinless second Adam, Jesus was man as God intended man to be. He then told us, "Do the works I have been doing" (John 14:12). John said those who "claim to live in him must live as Jesus did" (1 John 2:6). Paul understood this when he said, "Imitate me, just as I imitate Christ" (1 Cor. 11:1 NLT). Discipleship demands us to "follow" the resurrected Christ and "imitate" the priorities and patterns of the incarnate Christ. We like the expression "Jesus' model and method of disciple making" as a summary of what we do.

4. We believe love is the driving motive. The Great Commandment precedes the Great Commission. Loving God and loving people is the passion behind the priority, the motive behind the mission, the heart behind the hands. Love is the signature card of true disciples . . . disciple making cannot happen apart from loving and caring relationships . . . both tough and a tender love (1 Thess. 2). Larger ministries require more relational disciple makers to keep growing. Disciple making is relational and, as ministries grow, more relational disciples are needed. "By this everyone will know that you are my disciples, if you love one another" (John 13:35).

5. We believe verifiable fruit is the measure. God's agenda for each one of us is that we stay close to him and bear "fruit," "more fruit," and then ultimately "much fruit, showing yourselves to be my disciples" (John 15:8). God transforms our hearts as we "remain in [him]" and he leads us into lives of love (John 15:4, 17). Jesus modeled the focus of love as he came to seek, save, and disciple people (Luke 19:10; 6:40). Jesus masterfully showed how love produces disciples . . . reaching and developing his men and helping them grow from nonbelievers all the way to disciple makers reproducing disciple makers (Matt. 28:19–20). There is a natural process of moving people from those who do not know Jesus all the way to becoming mature disciple makers . . . and Jesus showed the model to us. In short, we haven't truly made mature disciples until they are following Jesus' model of love and helping to make more disciples . . . this is fruitful multiplication.

6. We believe Holy Spirit power is the means. Disciples cannot be made through fleshly efforts. Jesus, in his humanity, fully acknowledged his dependence on the Spirit. Disciple making is not just a good strategy . . . it is a way of life, accomplished through the fruit of the Holy Spirit living through a person's yielded and holy life (2 Cor. 3:16–17). If Jesus fully depended on the Holy Spirit's power, how can we do any less? The Holy Spirit will lead us to be obedient people who live holy lives to God's glory.

7. We believe the local church is the primary environment for disciple making. The church is for discipleship, and disciples manifest the kingdom of God to the world (Col. 1:28–29). When the church reverses this process and attempts to get the world to go to church instead of the church going to the world, you get chaos. Pastoral and ministerial work should be evaluated and rewarded based on how many

disciple makers are produced and the kind of people a church sends into the world. Jesus was a man for others; the church, likewise, is for others. Any plan that does not create disciples who live for others is a failure.

8. We believe that equipping leaders is the linchpin of the movement. All Christians are called to be disciples who grow to help make disciples, using the unique gifts God has given each of us. Leaders are also called to grow a movement of disciple making. This is called the church (2 Tim. 2:2). How Jesus built a movement differs from how Jesus made a disciple. If we are going to create a disciple-making movement in North America, it is our conviction we must train leaders in how Jesus built a movement. This is harder and takes more time, but in the end this will bear fruit that will remain. Practically, this means we must develop a team of disciple-making leaders (pastors), with various disciple-making best practices (church models), who can continue to fan the flame of disciple making.

9. We believe definitions are vitally important. (1) Our definition of disciple making—*helping people to trust and follow Jesus* (Matt. 28:18–20), which includes the whole process from conversion through maturation and multiplication; and (2) our definition of a **disciple**—*a person who is following Christ, being changed by Christ, and is committed to the mission of Christ* (Matt. 4:19 ESV).

10. We believe Jesus and Scripture are the basis. We believe the sixty-six books of the Bible are the authoritative, reliable, and ultimate standard for disciple making and life (2 Tim. 3:16–4:2) and that Jesus, as presented in the Bible and appropriately described by the Apostles' Creed and the Nicene Creed, rightfully deserves our focus and our commitment to a life of full discipleship.

■   ■   ■

We want to fan the flames, pour gasoline on the fires of this kind of disciple-making movement, and we hope that your heart resonates with ours. Making disciples of Jesus is God's strategy to heal and redeem the world. It is our conviction that a life well lived is a life devoted to this revolution. Won't you join us?

APPENDIX 2

Pastors and Church Planters
Who Make Disciple Makers

The following article first appeared in *Outreach Magazine* (September/October 2016), under the title "What Does It Take to Plant a Disciple-Making Church? Leading disciple makers share their five best multiplication practices" by Bobby Harrington.

For years I (Bobby) have served as the leader of the discipleship tracks at the annual *Exponential* church-planting conferences in addition to my work at discipleship.org. I have had the opportunity to bring together the nation's top disciple-making leaders to give them the opportunity to join their individual forces and focus on their common mission. As a result, I have been given a front-row

seat to listen in to their insights and learn what these world-changing ministries are doing to advance the Great Commission. The following points summarize the best disciple-making practices for planting churches that multiply disciples from day one.

1. THEY MAKE DISCIPLE MAKING THE TOP PRIORITY.

When Exponential Director Todd Wilson was writing the book *Becoming a Level 5 Multiplying Church*, we talked about the key factors behind Level 5 multiplication (new churches planting new churches). Todd focused on these churches' faith-filled leadership decisions. I focused on their discipleship practices. We agreed that such movements are also uniquely guided by the Holy Spirit and surmised that Level 5 churches come from 50 percent disciple-making practices, 25 percent leadership decisions, and 25 percent a miraculous move of the Holy Spirit. I felt good about our conclusions until I met Ralph Moore.

"I think disciple making is 90 percent of church multiplication," he told me. Moore pioneered the Hope Chapel movement, the clearest example of a Level 5 multiplication movement in North America. Hope Chapel now has a legacy of more than 2,300 churches. Moore's track record and reasoning are difficult to dispute.

Dann Spader of Sonlife Ministries and Global Youth Initiative is creating disciple-making movements in more than ninety countries. He describes leaders like Ralph Moore as "bleeders."

"They are so committed to disciple making that if you cut them, they will bleed it," Spader says. Discipleship author and speaker Bill Hull calls them "discipleship-first leaders."

However you describe it, disciple making is these leaders' top priority. They live it personally, talk about it regularly, and lead their church to make it an everyday reality. When fully embraced, disciple making turns a church into an incubator for multiplication, as this DNA creates micro-multiplication throughout the church. These leaders multiply everyday disciples who then become disciple makers and multiplying leaders. Many of these leaders naturally rise up to become church planters.

We see this kind of multiplication in the early church as Jesus invested in Peter, James, and John. We have the same potential today as leaders make disciple making their top priority.

2. THEY FOCUS ON EVERYDAY CHRISTIANS.

Too many times, we think that making disciples who make disciples requires a special type of leader and congregation. These national leaders continue to affirm that disciple-making churches start with everyday, ordinary people.

Jim Putman decided to plant a church and then moved to Post Falls, Idaho. He never finished his seminary degree, but he was committed to planting a church around Jesus' method of disciple making. He hoped that God would eventually bless his church with 200 to 300 people. Today, some 6,000 people gather at Real Life Ministries in a metropolitan area of about 40,000 people. Putman then helped launch the Relational Discipleship Network of churches with leaders who follow Jesus' method of disciple making—churches filled with everyday North Idaho people who have developed a core commitment to be disciples who make disciples where they live.

Most of the 90-plus pastoral staff at the church came to faith and eventually progressed to join the staff from *within* the church. These leaders started out as non-Christians who visited a small group and eventually decided to be baptized (typically by their small group leader). Soon, they began to lead a small group, followed by branching out to start a few new groups, then coaching small group leaders, and finally developing into disciple-making leaders who were ready to join the leadership staff now made up of former mill workers, former firefighters, and former business leaders.

Just like Jesus did with his fishermen-turned-followers, disciple-making leaders work to create cultures and support systems that equip and release people to be multipliers.

3. THEY KEEP IT SIMPLE.

The only way to plant and grow a church with everyday Christians actively making disciples is to make it simple. These leaders make it easy and reproducible.

Before moving to the United States, disciple-making leader Alex Absalom was part of one of the fastest-growing and largest churches in England. Along with missional leader Mike Breen and others, he developed a very simple disciple-making method. Together, they created missional communities (service communities) of 20 to 50 people and then broke those who were interested in going deeper into smaller groups of four to six people. The small groups became the engine of disciple making.

In those groups, leaders encouraged outside Bible reading, and each time the group met, they focused on two questions:

1. What is the Holy Spirit telling you?
2. What are you doing about what the Holy Spirit is telling you?

That's it. Boom! These groups began to multiply.

A few months ago, I asked Ralph Moore

to make a presentation on how disciple making worked in the Hope Chapel movement. He and Alex Absalom understand the importance and impact of simplicity:

"We invite people into relationships," Moore explained. "Then we invite them to our church gathering on Sunday where we preach one chapter from the Bible each week. From there, we have everyone get into a group in a home or coffee shop during the week, and each group follows the same format." Moore's groups ask three questions:

- What did the Holy Spirit tell you during the teaching Sunday?
- What are you doing about it?
- How can we help you by our prayers and support?

Hope Chapel small group leaders meet regularly with pastoral staff to work through leadership books and Scripture. In these leadership huddles, they ask the same three questions they ask in small groups, applying those questions to their leadership readings.

That's it. Simple. The heart of the Hope Chapel movement.

4. THEY PROVIDE PRACTICAL TOOLS.

Not all disciple-making leaders make it as stunningly simple as Absalom and Moore. But they do understand that equipping everyday Christians with practical disciple-making tools is key to multiplication.

Randy Pope is the founding pastor of Perimeter Church in Atlanta, part of the Presbyterian Church of America. Theology, Bible study, and doctrine are extremely important to the Atlanta church. So is church planting. Perimeter has planted 40 churches. Like all disciple-making churches, the church has a high number of people in discipling relationships outside of Sunday mornings, intentionally following Jesus' method of disciple making. Perimeter leaders have cracked the code on making deeper theology both practical and learnable. They call their model "Life on Life Missional Discipleship."

"Too many pastors talk about disciple making but fail their people because they do not give them practical, easily usable tools," Pope says, adding that tools are essential because they transform disciple making from an abstract concept or theory into natural, simple practices.

5. THEY MAKE "EQUIPPING CHRISTIANS FOR MINISTRY" THE TOP RESPONSIBILITY OF LEADERSHIP STAFF.

Don't miss this last practice. It is the foundation that supports the four practices above. Disciple-making leaders make sure ministerial staff know that it's their job to equip church members to do the ministry of the church. These national leaders agree that two roles are essential to creating a disciple-making, multiplying church: (1) pastoral leaders who function as equippers and (2) church members who function as ministers of the church.

Not only are disciple-making leaders committed to Jesus' method, they also are committed to being equippers of everyday Christians (Eph. 4:11–13 and 2 Tim. 2:2). The primary job of church leaders is to equip, train, and coach members to do the ministry of being disciples who make disciples.

Moreover, everyday church members must embrace their role. As the apostles Paul and Peter stress in their letters to the church, they are the ministers, serving God in their unique ministries (Rom. 12:3–8; 1 Peter 4:10–11).

When both roles are working together, a culture of multiplication begins to grow in which disciple-making leaders develop disciple makers who naturally develop disciples who grow to become disciple makers.

From these five best practices, we can develop a list of practical action points:

1. Become a leader who makes disciple making the top priority.
2. Focus on mobilizing everyday people.
3. Keep disciple making simple and reproducible.
4. Create practical tools that make disciple making doable.
5. Ask all staff to focus on equipping members to be disciple-making ministers.

Planting a church of disciples who make disciples isn't only doable; it is what Jesus commanded his church to do. When we make the multiplication of disciples our top priority, we lead and empower our present and future churches to find their place in Jesus' mission and his ultimate plan for redeeming his people.

NOTES

Chapter 1

1. See Bob Buford, *Halftime* (Grand Rapids: Zondervan, 1997), 53.
2. See Bill Hull, *Conversion and Discipleship: You Can't Have One without the Other* (Zondervan, 2016), in the "Ways and Means" chapter.
3. Many of our quotes from Dann Spader, Bill Hull, Jim Putman, Robert Coleman, and others come directly from talks we have had with them or things they have said in our presence or in our correspondence with them.
4. Bobby describes this shift in the book *Discipleship Is the Core Mission of the Church* (Exponential/discipleship.org, 2013), https://exponential.org/resource-ebooks/discipleship-core/.
5. Dallas Willard has a wonderful book on the importance of love to biblical faithfulness. See *Getting Love Right* (Amazon Digital, 2012).

Chapter 2

1. We borrowed this from Max Lucado. See Max Lucado, *And the Angels Were Silent* (Sisters, OR: Multnomah, 1992).
2. We are indebted to Jim Putman for championing

this definition of a disciple. For more information on this definition, see Jim Putman and Bobby Harrington, *DiscipleShift: Five Steps That Help Your Church to Make Disciples Who Make Disciples* (Grand Rapids: Zondervan, 2013).

3. We prefer "disciple making" to "discipleship." The word *discipleship* describes the *state of being a disciple*. It is often used as a synonym for *disciple making*. We have no quibble with those who use it that way when they carefully define what it means, but we prefer to use the expression *disciple making* when describing how we help people trust and follow Jesus. Dann Spader has spent his life helping people emulate Jesus' method and model of disciple making through Sonlife Ministries and Global Youth Initiative. He now works in over ninety countries training Christian leaders to follow Jesus. He has persuaded us that it is important to emphasize the expression *disciple making* because it communicates a focus on *what Jesus did with his disciples and the words of Matthew 28:19*. Jesus made disciples and commanded us to make disciples with an assumption that

we would do it the way Jesus did it. Too often church leaders have a preconception when the word *discipleship* is used. In the past it meant Bible study or doctrine or training in the facts of the faith. These are all important elements, and they are important parts of making disciples. But they tend to restrict the focus in people's minds to books, classes, and memorization. It is often an unhealthy overemphasis on education and Bible study. They are an important part of what we want to emphasize, but there is much more. Jesus' emphasis was a little broader. Jesus' style of disciple making accentuated relationships. Jesus also went beyond the transfer of information (which was an important part of what he did with the disciples) to include coaching and real-life application. It was life on life. It was up close and personal. Again, we are big proponents of Bible study, and we still use the word *discipleship*. But disciple making may be a more helpful expression because it calls us to focus on what Jesus did, and it helps us delineate it from an overemphasis on just Bible education.

4. R. T. France, *The Gospel of Matthew,* The New International Commentary on the New Testament (Grand Rapids: Eerdmans, 2007), 114–17.

5. We find Randy Alcorn's *The Grace and Truth Paradox: Responding with Christlike Balance* (Sisters, OR: Multnomah, 2003) to be a very practical paradigm along these lines, especially for the local church.

6. See Bill Hull and Bobby Harrington, *Evangelism or Discipleship: Can They Effectively Work Together?* (Exponential and discipleship.org, 2014).

7. Bill Hull, *Conversion and Discipleship: You Can't Have One without the Other* (Grand Rapids: Zondervan, 2016).

8. See the latest example by N. T. Wright, *Simply Good News: Why the Gospel Is News and What Makes It Good* (New York: HarperOne, 2015).

9. For more on this framework, see Putman and Harrington, *DiscipleShift: Five Steps That Help Your Church to Make Disciples Who Make Disciples.*

10. We have worked with a lot of church leaders around North America and many international ones too. We have yet to find anyone who does not look to Coleman's work as the definitive work on Jesus' method. See Robert Coleman, *The Master Plan of Evangelism* (Grand Rapids: Revell, 1963).

11. Robert Coleman and Bobby Harrington with Josh Patrick, *Revisiting the Master Plan of Evangelism: Why Jesus' Discipleship Method Is Still the Best Today* (Exponential and discipleship.org, 2014). www.discipleship.org.

12. Jim Putman, *The Power of Together* (Grand Rapids: Baker, 2016).

13. We want to acknowledge the group of national leaders we worked with through discipleship.org to create the framework of the seven elements. The group included Robert Coleman, Bill Hull, Dann Spader, Jim Putman, Francis Chan, Jeff Vanderstelt, Kennon Vaughan, Robby Gallaty, Leon Drennan, and especially the creative designer Josh Shank, along with others.

Chapter 3

1. We took this from Dann Spader, *4 Chair Discipling: Growing a Movement of Disciple-Makers* (Chicago: Moody, 2014).

Chapter 4

1. Robert Coleman and Bobby Harrington, with Josh Patrick, *Revisiting the Master Plan of Evangelism: Why Jesus' Discipleship Method Is Still the*

Best Today (Exponential and discipleship.org, 2014). www.discipleship.org.

2. Ibid., 11.

3. See Jim Putman, *The Power of Together* (Grand Rapids: Baker, 2016), for a wonderful book on the topic of this chapter.

4. Eugene Peterson, *The Jesus Way* (Grand Rapids: Eerdmans, 2007), 1.

5. Neal Gabler, "Commentary: The Social Networks," *Los Angeles Times* (October 17, 2010), http://articles.latimes.com/2010/oct/17/entertainment/la-ca-tv-friendships-20101017.

6. See M. Scott Boren, *The Relational Way* (Houston: Touch, 2007).

7. One of the best proponents of this idea is Robert Banks, *Paul's Idea of Community* (Grand Rapids: Baker Academic, 1994). See L. Coenen, "Church," in *The New International Dictionary of the New Testament,* ed. Colin Brown (Grand Rapids: Zondervan, 1975), 1: 291–307.

8. See Wesley Hill, *Spiritual Friendship* (Grand Rapids: Brazos, 2015) and spiritualfriendship.org.

9. For example, Jim Putman and Bobby Harrington, *DiscipleShift: Five Steps That Help Your Church to Make Disciples Who Make Disciples* (Grand Rapids: Zondervan, 2013).

10. Special thanks to Virgil Grant for his input on this list.

Chapter 5

1. Mauro Pianta, "U2's Bono says 'Jesus was the Son of God or he was nuts,'" *Vatican Insider,* April 15, 2014, http://www.preachingtoday.com/illustrations/2014/may/?start=21, accessed June 16, 2016.

2. See how Hull unpacks all the implications of this statement in his book *Conversion and Discipleship: You Can't Have One Without the Other* (Grand Rapids: Zondervan, 2016).

3. We slightly tweaked DeYoung's statements. See https://blogs.thegospelcoalition.org/kevindeyoung/2014/11/20/who-do-you-say-i-am/.

4. See Everett Ferguson, *The Rule of Faith: A Guide* (Eugene, OR: Wipf and Stock, 2015), and Philip Schaff, *The Creeds of Christendom, Volume 1: The History of the Creeds,* reprint, Kindle ed. (n.a.: Laconia, 2016).

5. See also Mark 2:1–12; John 10:29–39; 20:28; 2 Corinthians 5:19; Philippians 2:5–11; Colossians 1:15–20; 2:9; Hebrews 1:6–8; Revelation 1:17, 20; 22:13. An excellent discussion of Christ's nature is also found in John Stott, *Basic Christianity* (London: InterVarsity, 1958).

6. We commend the broad outline of Scot McKnight's *The King Jesus Gospel: The Original Good News Revisited,* Revised Edition (Grand Rapids: Zondervan, 2011) and *Kingdom Conspiracy: Returning to the Radical Mission of the Local Church* (Grand Rapids: Brazos, 2014).

7. Bill Hull describes the importance of this broader paradigm in *Christlike: The Pursuit of Uncomplicated Obedience* (Colorado Springs: NavPress, 2010), 44.

8. See N. T. Wright, *Simply Good News: Why the Gospel Is News and What Makes It Good* (New York: HarperOne, 2015).

9. Bill Hull, *Conversion and Discipleship: You Can't Have One without the Other* (Grand Rapids: Zondervan, 2016).

10. A. T. Robertson, *Word Pictures in the New Testament,* Volume 4 (Grand Rapids: Baker Book House, 1990), 525.

11. Michka Assayas, *Bono: In Conversation with Michka Assayas* (New York: Riverhead, 2005), submitted by Van Morris, Mt. Washington, Kentucky.

12. See David Platt, *Follow Me: A Call to Die. A Call to Live.* (Carol Stream, IL: Tyndale, 2013),

and Robert Picirilli, *Discipleship: The Expression of Saving Faith* (Nashville: Randall, 2013).

13. Ibid.

14. John MacArthur, *The Gospel According to Jesus* (Grand Rapids: Zondervan, 1988), 178.

15. See Platt, *Follow Me: A Call to Die. A Call to Live,* and Picirilli, *Discipleship: The Expression of Saving Faith.*

16. As late as 2010, up to 85 percent of Americans claimed to be Christian, though by 2015 it had fallen to 76 percent. See George Barna, *Futurecast* (Carol Stream, IL: Tyndale, 2011), Kindle location 124. See also The Navigators, *The State of Discipleship* (Carol Stream, IL: Tyndale, 2015).

17. Ed Stetzer, "Barna: How Many Have a Biblical Worldview," *Christianity Today* (March 9, 2009), http://www.christianitytoday.com/edstetzer/2009/march/barna-how-many-have-biblical-worldview.html.

Chapter 6

1. *Oxford Dictionaries,* s.v. "intentionality," http://oxforddictionaries.com/us/definition/ american _english/intentionality, accessed September 23, 2013.

2. For more information on the disappearance of moral knowledge, see Dallas Willard, *Knowing Christ Today: Why We Can Trust Spiritual Knowledge* (New York: HarperCollins, 2009).

3. The participles in verse 19 are subordinate to the imperative command "make disciples," and they explain how disciples are made: "baptizing" them and "teaching" them obedience to all of Jesus' commandments. See Craig Blomberg, *Matthew: An Exegetical and Theological Exposition of Holy Scripture,* The New American Commentary (Nashville, Broadman, 1992), 431.

4. J. A. Thompson, *Deuteronomy* (London: InterVarsity, 1974).

5. Jason Houser, Bobby Harrington, and Chad Harrington, *Dedicated: Training Your Children to Trust and Follow Jesus* (Grand Rapids: Zondervan, 2015).

6. Peter Craige, *The Book of Deuteronomy* (Grand Rapids: Eerdmans, 1976), 170.

7. See Robert Coleman, *The Master Plan of Evangelism* (Grand Rapids: Revell, 1963).

8. No one seems to know where this poem originally came from. It can be found at http://jayemartin.blogspot.com/2011/03/what-is-gospel-according-to-you.html.

Chapter 7

1. Almost every in-depth analysis of the state of discipleship in the church today points to the supreme need for people to get into the Word of God and apply it to their lives. See Eric Geiger, Michael Kelley, and Philip Nation, *Transformational Discipleship: How People Really Grow* (Nashville: B&H, 2012), Kindle locations 910–18. Bill Hybels summarizes the results of the massive REVEAL studies: "We learned that the most effective strategy for moving people forward in their journey of faith is biblical engagement. Not just getting people into the Bible when they're in church—which we do quite well—but helping them engage the Bible on their own outside of church." See in Greg Hawkins and Cally Parkinson, *Move: What 1,000 Churches Reveal about Spiritual Growth* (Grand Rapids: Zondervan, 2011), Kindle location 71–72.

2. Harpeth Church has study guides for those who want to disciple nonbelievers. I (Bobby) really like Robby Gallaty's model in his book *Growing Up: How to Be a Disciple Who Makes

Disciples (Bloomington, IN: Crossbook, 2013). We also like Neil Cole's "Life Transformation Groups" described in *Search & Rescue: Becoming a Disciple Who Makes a Difference* (Grand Rapids: Baker, 2008). See also the good material at the First Steps website, http://stores2.faithhighway.com/Merchant5/merchant.mvc?Screen=SFNT&Store_ Code =FSM&Category_Code=STFTP.

3. Jesus Is Savior.com, http://www.jesus-is-savior .com/Great%20Men%20of%20God/dwight _moody-quotes.htm, accessed October 1, 2013.

4. Quoted in Michael Green, ed., *Illustrations for Biblical Preaching* (Grand Rapids: Baker, 1989), 30.

5. Alister McGrath shows the importance of this and how to do it in our world today in *A Passion for Truth: The Intellectual Coherence of Evangelicalism* (Downers Grove, IL: InterVarsity, 1996).

6. Quoted in Green, ed., *Illustrations for Biblical Preaching*, 35.

7. Contact discipleship.org for these materials.

8. This book by Bobby Harrington and Alex Absalom, *Discipleship That Fits: The Five Kinds of Relationships God Uses to Help Us Grow* (Grand Rapids: Zondervan, 2016) provides a good list of material that can be helpful for disciple makers.

Chapter 9

1. See Avery Willis, Jim Putman, Brandon Guindon, and Bill Krause, *Real-Life Discipleship Training Manual: Equipping Disciples Who Make Disciples* (Colorado Springs: NavPress, 2010).

2. See ibid. This manual is the most helpful tool we have found for training disciple makers. There is no substitute for working through this manual to help you know how to disciple people in practical terms. At Harpeth Church, we require all of our small group leaders to work through this manual and be thoroughly trained in the process and journey of discipleship.

Chapter 10

1. See James Fleming, *Turning Points in the Life of Jesus* (LaGrange, GA: Biblical Resources, 1999), 47ff. Fleming also marks this as one of the key turning points in Jesus' life.

2. Dave Ferguson and Jon Ferguson, *Exponential: How You and Your Friends Can Start a Missional Church Movement* (Grand Rapids: Zondervan, 2010).

3. Tony Campolo, *Let Me Tell You a Story* (Nashville: Nelson, 2000).

4. William G. McLoughlin, *Revivals, Awakenings, and Reform: An Essay on Religion and Social Change in America, 1607–1977* (Chicago: University of Chicago Press, 1980), 144.

5. C. H. Spurgeon, *The Soul Winner,* reprint ed. (New Kensington, PA: Whitaker, 1995), 233.

6. Ibid., 203–4.

7. Russ Busby, *Billy Graham: God's Ambassador* (Minneapolis: Billy Graham Evangelistic Association, 1999), 1.

Conclusion

1. See the prayer of Patrick at http://www .goodreads.com/quotes/413139-christ-with-me -christ-before-me-christ-behind-me-christ.

CPSIA information can be obtained
at www.ICGtesting.com
Printed in the USA
JSHW050329100623
42968JS00002B/3